Praise for *Doctors Cry, Too*

~ ✤ ~

"Dr. Boehm has used a lifetime of experience in medicine to create a prescription for life we can all use. I cried, too."
— **Art Ulene, M.D.**, America's family doctor

"A loving and lovely book. It will remind patients to see their doctors as human beings and remind doctors of their obligation to be human beings first."
— **Rabbi Harold Kushner**, author of
When Bad Things Happen to Good People

*"I believe that **Doctors Cry, Too** makes an important contribution toward guiding physicians, as well as others in the helping professions, to recognize their personal feelings of compassion without interfering with their professional responsibilities. I read this book with great interest and found it to be thought-provoking."*
— **Dr. Ruth Westheimer**, author and TV personality

"Boehm's stories are filled with examples of what can happen when compassion is a part of the process. . . . This book should be read by every present and future doctor and every patient."
— **Bernie Siegel, M.D.**, author of *Love, Medicine & Miracles* and *Prescriptions for Living*

DOCTORS CRY, TOO

Hay House Titles of Related Interest

YOU CAN HEAL YOUR LIFE, the movie, starring Louise Hay & Friends
(available as a 1-DVD program, an expanded 2-DVD set,
and an online streaming video)
Learn more at www.hayhouse.com/louise-movie

THE SHIFT, the movie, starring Dr. Wayne W. Dyer
(available as a 1-DVD program, an expanded 2-DVD set,
and an online streaming video)
Learn more at www.hayhouse.com/the-shift-movie

BOOKS

A Journal of Love and Healing: Transcending Grief,
by Sylvia Browne and Nancy Dufresne

Practical Parenting, by Montel Williams and Jeffrey Gardère, Ph.D.

The Reconnection: Heal Others, Heal Yourself, by Dr. Eric Pearl

Roots of Healing: The New Medicine, by Andrew Weil, M.D.,
and Other Contributors

AUDIO PROGRAMS

*Healing and Spirituality: The Sacred Quest for Transformation
of Body and Soul,* by Joan Borysenko, Ph.D.

Meditations for Overcoming Life's Stresses and Strains,
by Bernie Siegel, M.D.

DOCTORS CRY, TOO

Essays from the Heart of a Physician

Frank H. Boehm, M.D.

Hay House, Inc.
Carlsbad, California • New York City
London • Sydney • New Delhi

Published in the United States by: Hay House, Inc., www.hayhouse.com
Published in Australia by: Hay House Australia Ltd. www.hayhouse.com.au
Published in the United Kingdom by: Hay House UK, Ltd. www.hayhouse.co.uk
Published in India by: Hay House Publishers India, www.hayhouse.co.in

Editorial supervision: Jill Kramer • *Design:* Summer McStravick

Library of Congress Cataloging-in-Publication Data
for the Original Edition

Boehm, Frank H.
    Doctors cry, too : essays from the heart of a physician / by Frank H. Boehm ; with a foreword by John L. Seigenthaler.
        p. cm.
    ISBN 1-56170-816-X (hardcover) • 1-4019-0129-8 (tradepaper)
    1. Physicians—Anecdotes. 2. Medicine—Anecdotes. I. Title.

R705 .B655 2001
610.69'6—dc21

00-054020

Tradepaper ISBN: 978-1-4019-6279-1
E-book ISBN: 9781-4019-2977-0

1st edition, August 2001
2nd edition, September 2003
3rd edition, September 2020

Printed in the United States of America

*This book is dedicated to
my wife, Julie, the love of my life—
my critic, advisor, and best friend*

and

*in memory of Artie Pine—
for his vision and belief in me*

❀ ❀ ❀

Contents

~ ❦ ~

Foreword

There is something oxymoronic about the thought of doctors being in tears over the emotional torment their patients suffer when health problems are serious. It is an image out of sync with what public opinion polls tell us about doctor-patient relationships. Many U.S. citizens think that, as a group, physicians are insensitive, unsympathetic, and unresponsive when health crises arise. They seem anesthetized to emotion.

That is one side of the health-care coin. The other side is that patients also say they feel close bonds with their personal physicians—even though they resent not being able to communicate more fully with them. They get agitated and angry when some HMO administrator tells them that they cannot continue to see the doctor who had treated them for years.

We live in a time when almost every institution is subject to a massive dose of cynicism. We don't trust our politicians, our journalists, our lawyers, our police officers, our schoolteachers, our librarians, our real estate brokers, our car dealers, our garbage collectors; or even many of our preachers, priests, and rabbis whose pulpit pronouncements sound too conservative or too liberal.

Is the doctor-patient relationship, then, really so important? Does it matter if patients don't trust the members of the American Medical Association or the plenitude of other alphabet-soup societies of physicians?

In fact, it *should* matter. The continuing high cost of health care makes it important. The revolutionary break-throughs in scientific research, diagnostic technology, so-called miracle drugs, and novel operative procedures make it important. The laws, regulations, policies, standards, and court rulings that have created ethical dilemmas for the men and women of the medical community make it important. The political and religious controversies that swirl around the physician-patient connection make it important.

Virtually every U.S. citizen's link with physicians stretches from birth to death; cradle to grave. Most of us breathed our first breath at the touch of a physician's hand. For many of us, the doctor's touch will be one of the last we sense. Between birth and death, we rely on doctors to heal our bodies and minds, sharing with them along the way some of the most sensitive secrets of the soul.

And whatever cynical sentiments we may hold for others who seek to serve us, down deep we do trust our men and women of medicine. When our doctor asks how we feel, we respond differently than to anybody else who might ask the same question on a given day. We tell our doctors exactly how we feel in depth and in detail, sometimes with fear and pas-sion. We want them to talk to us.

When illnesses create uncertainty and stress, patients need more than explanations. They seek a measure of comfort, a bit of shared knowledge, a little wisdom. That is what they get from Frank Boehm in this telling and timely book of essays about his practice, his profession, his peers, and himself.

As the world of medicine has become more complex, more commercial, and more multifaceted, Dr. Boehm has sought to create a bridge of comprehension across the grow-ing chasm of patient ignorance and misunderstanding.

For most of the last decade, his newspaper column, "Heal-ing Words," has combined his talent as a writer and his skill as a physician to make sense out of the confounding health-care conundrums that inevitably cross the public mind. *Doctors Cry, Too* is a fascinating collection of more than 60 of those columns dealing with issues of interest including depression, life and death, happiness and grief, and much more.

Boehm, unlike many of his peers, has found a way to communicate. He writes with drops of humor, doses of pathos, and a diet of common sense as a prescription to enlighten as well as entertain.

He is not afraid to use an implausible rhetorical line to grab the attention or capture the imagination of readers. An example is his suggestion that "doctors cry, too." His point is not that his peers love our livers and limbs and breasts and bones and colons and cartilage, or even that they love us—but they *relate* to us. They are *concerned* about us. They hurt when we hurt. But many of them have been trained to internalize emotion.

He recognizes that some doctors too often mask the depth of their feelings, stifle demonstrations of concern, and submerge all but superficial expressions of sympathy. He is convinced that they thereby deny their patients needed solace, and themselves the opportunity to be seen as they really are—caring as well as curing, humane as well as human.

Also, he offers a line of hope. A younger generation of doctors—men and women who enter the practice to help sick people—are presenting themselves as more demonstrative, more engaging, and more involved with their patients.

It is also refreshing to hear from a doctor that everything he has learned about his business did not come from the classroom or lab. Patients, colleagues, relatives, and friends have helped teach Frank Boehm how to be a good doctor: a pregnant woman with cancer, a ten-year-old boy with congenital heart disease, a child on an airplane, a mother giving birth to quintuplets, a woman who miscarried, a nosy reporter at an Academy Awards ceremony—each anecdote is a story with a moral.

From his father, Ludwig, Frank learned that forgiveness heals; from his mother-in-law, Dorothy, he learned on her deathbed the power of the human spirit to end her life as she had lived it; from his mother, Ilse, he discovered that grief can be a killing illness; from patients whose cures defied rational medical explanation, he acknowledges a power larger than life.

Frank Boehm is barely old enough (and I am *more* than old enough) to remember a time when doctors actually made house calls, a time when the sick stayed home in bed and the doctor drove himself to the patient's residence to diagnose illness, prescribe treatment, and even to dispense drugs. In our home, when the physician's bedside visit was concluded, there was often coffee and cake, perhaps even a cocktail, and always conversational chitchat with members of the patient's family. It was "get-acquainted" time.

That may sound like the good old days of American medicine to some. But in fact, for all the perceived and real faults and foibles of the profession—not to mention the high cost of care—we actually now live in the best days in the history of our nation's health. Still, we yearn for that conversational chitchat of the past that enriched our knowledge of what ailed us, built our trust in American medicine, and left us with the certain knowledge that our doctors cared.

In a real sense, Frank Boehm's essays are surrogate house calls.

Hidden between the lines of many of them are two simple messages about life-or-death issues.

To patients, he says, "Your doctors really care about you."
To doctors, he says, "Show them you really care."

— **John L. Seigenthaler**

John L Seigenthaler founded the First Amendment Center at Vanderbilt University in Nashville. A former president of the American Society of Newspaper Editors, he served for 43 years as an award-winning journalist for *The Tennessean,* Nashville's morning newspaper. He retains the title *chairman emeritus* of *The Tennessean.*

In 1982, John became founding editorial director of *USA Today* and served in that position for a decade, retiring from both the Nashville and national newspapers in 1991. Currently, John hosts a weekly book-review program, "A Word on Words," which is distributed through the Southern Public Television Network. He is a member of the boards of trustees of The Freedom Forum and the First Amendment Center.

Preface

*F*or years, many of my readers have asked me when I planned to put my columns into a book. My answer has always been the same: "Soon."

However, my delay over the past nine years since my twice-a-month op-ed column, "Healing Words," appeared in *The Tennessean*, has been in determining what direction my book should take. After several versions, I concluded that what my readers wanted are stories that deal with the emotional and personal issues surrounding health care and physicians.

In putting this book together, I have selected essays that have been some of my readers' favorites (however, I should note that they're not in any type of chronological order, necessarily). They include special moments in my life, such as my son and daughter going off to college, coping with the personal grief of losing loved ones, the birth of my granddaughter, and the healing that comes from joy. They address my point of view on such subjects as strength and courage, faith, happiness, depression, forgiveness, death and dying, friendship, the heartbreak of infertility, parenting, and the physician/patient bond. These essays also reveal the humanistic, emotional, and compassionate side of physicians as they go about the enormously complicated task of healing the sick.

By gaining insight into the heart of *one* physician, it is my hope that you, the reader, will gain insight into the heart of *many* physicians.

Acknowledgments

I want to thank the many readers who have supported me through the years by reading my columns and letting me know their thoughts and opinions. I wish to thank *The Tennessean*'s editor, Frank Sutherland, for extending the offer to Dr. John Sergent and me to author our weekly column titled "Healing Words," and for being supportive of my efforts from the very beginning. I also want to express my appreciation for the help and advice I have received over the years from *The Tennessean*'s editorial editor, Frank Ritter. His calm, supportive manner is appreciated.

Thank you to Randall Murray, the *Boca News* editor, who enabled my words to move beyond Nashville . . . and into the hands and heart of literary agent Arthur Pine, who had faith in my writing ability, and whose willingness to take a chance on an unknown writer led me to my publisher, Hay House, and my editor, Jill Kramer, who took what I had and made it better. And, my sincerest thanks to Richard Pine for his support throughout this project.

To Reid Tracy, Jacqui Clark, and Tonya Toone, who provided their expertise and friendship in equal measure, I owe a world of debt.

Most of all, I wish to thank my wife, Julie, for encouraging my dream and never letting me give up. Her critiques, suggestions, and comments have helped smooth over each and every story, and her editorial style allowed for essays that are easy to read, understand, and digest. Her advice and hard work in putting this book together has been immeasurable.

To my patients who have allowed me to participate in their health care and to be a part of their lives, I owe an incredible debt. Many of my columns were born through their joys and sorrows. To my friends whose insights and suggestions have served as the catalyst for many of my stories, I am eternally grateful. And to those special friends and family who read my manuscript, your comments proved invaluable.

Last, I feel privileged to have been able to work by the side of my fellow doctors. It is from them that I learned the most. Physicians are a dedicated, hardworking, and compassionate group. To them I acknowledge a deep sense of appreciation and thanks for all they taught me and the inspiration I gain daily from working in their presence.

Introduction

By comparative standards, I certainly was not a brilliant child. While I held my own throughout high school, college challenged me in ways I had not anticipated. Yet, despite my lack of brilliance, I felt that I would be a good physician and would enjoy the world of medicine more than any other occupation I had considered.

If not brilliant, I was at least different. Born to German-Jewish immigrants who left Nazi Germany in 1938, and raised in an extended home-type atmosphere in a small southern town with aunts, uncles, cousins, and grandparents, I was not your typical southern boy.

I am not quite sure when I first decided to make medicine my career, but it started somewhere with the purchase of a chemistry set at age 14, and became absolute upon realizing that young, attractive girls and their mothers were considerably more responsive when I told them of my desire to become a physician.

I knew one thing during those unusual, turbulent, pimple-faced, insecure years of adolescence: I wanted to make something of myself. So when I walked to the mailbox that day in April many years ago and opened the envelope that contained my acceptance to medical school, I knew—although I was only 20 years old—that I had been given a key, one that would open doors of knowledge, excitement, fulfillment, and pleasure. The rest was up to me.

Growing up, my exposure to physicians had been positive. I vividly remember my mother getting me out of my sick bed, putting me in an uncomfortable chair while she changed my sheets, and straightened up in anticipation of the doctor's house call.

The genteel, bespectacled pediatrician had a kind voice, soft hands, and a warm manner, and I liked him very much. My family's respect for him was obvious, too, and when news of his death reached me many years later, I was saddened.

Although there has been a changing attitude toward physicians over the past 50 years, doctors still maintain a warm spot in the hearts of many of their patients, similar to how my family felt about our own doctor. We are also witnessing a vast improvement in the overall health of most Americans when compared to the status of their health in the 1940s.

Yet, despite these attitudes, as well as advances in modern medicine, there has been an erosion in the perception of the medical profession—and problems with health-care reform and increasing medical malpractice claims are only a few of the symptoms. Some other areas of frustration include resentment when things do not go well medically or surgically, impatience over filled waiting rooms coupled with long waits and short visits with the physician, and, of course, soaring costs.

However, I have always been intrigued by the fact that while people often find fault with the medical profession as a whole, they are less critical and usually quite benevolent in their comments about their own personal physicians. Perhaps this can be attributed to the one-on-one relationship, where the physician can display the kind of concern, warmth, sincerity, and knowledge that patients so eagerly desire. Thus, a bond of trust develops that builds over the years. A physician is often looked upon as a friend and partner to help their patients down life's path.

In some instances, the doctor is unable to reveal his or her compassionate side, and the patient is left with fears and questions. While I have come to realize that the humanistic qualities of all physicians are not always apparent, I believe that feelings of sympathy, worry, and concern for our patients is inherent in most of us.

Fortunately, with the introduction of a more sensitive and open approach to teaching and practicing medicine, I have noticed that our new doctors are more able and willing to reveal their emotions to their patients. And, being both a participant and observer in the myriad dramas of the medical world on a daily basis, I see tears glisten in the eyes of physicians as patients entrust their lives to us during life's many painful moments.

Writing my column has been great fun and a true labor of love. Reading over the essays once again to determine which ones to include in this book, I am reminded of each specific individual, event, or patient who inspired the copy.

It is my hope that *Doctors Cry, Too* will help you understand that physicians are subject to the same stresses and pressures of life—and are struggling with many of the same difficult and perplexing issues—as everyone else.

Despite what you may think of us as a group, after studying, working, and living with my colleagues and friends over the past 35 years, I can assure you that . . . *doctors cry, too!*

~ PART I

The Emotional and Spiritual Side

In the early days of our medical-school training, we physicians are taught the science of medicine. We dissect cadavers to learn how human bodies are put together; and we learn the basics of biochemistry, physiology, histology, and pathology. Finally, we are brought to the patient's bedside to apply all that we have learned.

It is there that we realize that the science of medicine cannot teach us all we need to know. It is at the bedside that we learn humility, wonder, and awe. This is where we experience the emotional and spiritual side of the profession we call medicine.

Miracle Department

DOCTORS DO NOT OFTEN discuss religion with their patients or among themselves.

That may seem odd when you consider that so much of what we physicians do involves or evokes a spiritual or religious feeling. Our patients pray for well-being and a favorable outcome. They put their faith in us, and in their God, as they go through the rigors laid out before them in their endeavor to regain health. Families hold prayer sessions, and patients make peace with themselves, their family, and their Higher Power, and then ask, "Why?"

As physicians (although we may not vocalize this sentiment), we feel a particular awe and responsibility about our chosen profession as we go about our daily business. That sense of wonder (and occasional fear) that we often experience inspires a feeling of closeness with a spiritual presence that many of us call God.

A call late one summer evening offered me an opportunity to reflect on this aspect of medicine. As I drove at breakneck speed down a narrow road to the labor-and-delivery room, I recalled the words spoken by an intern over the phone: "Dr. B., please hurry. A patient is dying."

I dreaded the implications and knew I needed to move quickly. Little else could be elicited via telephone without losing precious seconds, so I found myself hurtling toward this crisis, not knowing what I would find or what role I would play.

Rushing through the familiar procedure of changing into scrubs, then pushing my way through doors labeled "Absolutely No Admittance," I noticed the lack of staff at the nursing station. This was a bad sign. They were all in the delivery room dealing with the crisis.

As I quickly moved through the last door, I realized that only my body had passed through the doorway, leaving my hand behind. The ring on my left hand had caught the latch, and with a violent jolt, I was brought to my knees.

I lay there, the world spinning around me, with no help in sight—only the silence of the room and the panic in my soul. My ring had torn through the flesh of my finger, and a throbbing pain pierced my consciousness as the ring made contact with the underlying bone.

I attempted to regain composure, removing the ring from my finger as it began to swell to twice its normal size. Splashing water on my face, I knew I was in trouble. Someone's life depended on me, yet my head was spinning, my knees were shaking, and my heart was pounding.

Somehow I reached the operating room, and moments later made a quick diagnosis and began opening the patient's abdomen from chest to pubic bone, without even knowing her name. Blood was everywhere. The woman, who had just delivered a healthy baby girl, had ruptured an aneurysm (an abnormal weakened bulge in an artery) of her right kidney artery.

Few survive this tragic event, and if she were to live, speed was of the essence. Using my peripheral vision, I took in the activities in the room. Anesthesiologists were pumping two lines of blood into the patient while moving rapidly behind a screen to monitor the many vital signs that needed careful attention. Nurses were scurrying around bringing equipment to the table, changing the lights and helping wherever required. Pediatricians stood by the newborn, waiting for an appropriate time to exit; and medical students, interns, and residents gathered.

Despite all this intensity, the room was quiet—an eerie quiet that seemed to echo: "This is it; this is what we are all about."

Then, with three surgical assistants aiding me, I held the patient's aorta, compressing it as best I could to keep the blood from pouring out of the ruptured vessel. With my right hand, I had reached the area of the bleeding vessel that desperately needed a clamp.

Once applied, the bleeding would cease, the emergency would end, and a routine procedure would follow. Yet despite my years of training and experience, I could not position the clamp accurately because my swollen, throbbing left hand was unable to compress the huge aorta.

I knew that each second counted and that if I failed at my attempt, this new mother would die. I silently mumbled words of prayer: *I need help, and I need it now.* It was at that moment that something extraordinary happened.

Suddenly, out of the crowd of spectators, a sterilized instrument was passed to our arena of life and death. "Try this" were the words I heard coming from a seasoned surgical resident.

He had rushed to the operating suite a floor below and had brought back an aorta compressor used frequently by surgeons dealing in trauma, but employed little by OB/GYNs.

Properly placing the aorta compressor, the surgical field became visible. The abnormal opening of the renal artery was identified, clamped, and repaired, and the crisis ended almost as quickly as it had begun. Our patient survived, personnel and spectators departed the room, and I was left with a few of my remaining crew to close the incision.

Later, wiping the sweat from my brow and attempting to endure the pain emanating from my left hand, I knew that I had contacted God. I was very thankful. The teamwork in *this* world, coupled with the added presence of the Spirit in all of us did its job well.

❧ ❧ ❧

Was It Prayer or Medicine?

RELIGION HAS ALWAYS fascinated me.

As a child, I can vividly remember my parents and grandparents involving me in spiritually oriented activities, encouraging me to study my religion and to get involved with our house of worship. As I grew older, my interest in religion grew, and had it not been for my love of science, I might well have become a man of the cloth.

It is not surprising, then, that I still maintain an interest in my own faith, and in others' as well. Religion and medicine form a powerful union. I often see patients turn to religion at times of ill health, and prayer is often the tool that patients use to help bring them comfort and hope during troubled times.

I've often wondered about prayer. Can we *pray* for good health, or is prayer better used for inward reflection, providing inner strength during trying times? Can prayer influence the outcome of disease? Does it really make a difference?

While my medical training makes me somewhat skeptical of prayer as a process that can alter the inevitable, I have witnessed circumstances that have caused me to look beyond medical facts.

It was approximately 14 years ago that a patient of mine delivered a child who, because of a severe blood disorder, was given no hope of surviving. Five days after the baby's birth, the pediatrician told me that he was discontinuing the child's ventilator support system. He was absolutely certain that due to failing lungs and a malfunctioning heart, death would come soon thereafter.

As I walked toward my patient's room that morning, I searched to find the proper words to explain what was happening to her newborn child, and to express my sympathy. I was not given a chance to do either.

Filling the small hospital room and totally surrounding my patient's bed, an assortment of men and women stood silently, holding each others' hands and praying with bowed heads and closed eyes. The minister, small in stature, could hardly be seen as he uttered soothing words of prayer from a nearby corner.

I stood motionless in the doorway, transfixed by this scene. Finally, they were all finished and, upon noticing me, my patient smiled and said, "Don't worry, Dr. Boehm, our entire town is at church this very moment lifting their prayers to God. We will be heard."

The following morning, I left for a week-long vacation. Upon returning, I asked my pediatric colleague what had happened to the child I had delivered two weeks earlier. "Look over there," he said, pointing to an infant being bottle-fed by a nurse in the normal nursery area. "I can't explain it; I was so sure he couldn't live in his condition."

Several times since that day at the hospital, I have witnessed similar "miracles" and have often wondered if these were also examples of the power of prayer, or just reminders of how limited doctors are in their knowledge of life and death.

Perhaps it's a little of both.

Finding Strength

THE YOUNG COUPLE SITTING IN MY OFFICE looked panicked.

They had been referred to me because an obstetric ultrasound examination performed several days earlier on the expectant mother had revealed a serious fetal malformation, spina bifida, and hydrocephaly. The woman's pregnancy was in its seventh month, and her physician believed that she and her unborn child would benefit from care by a high-risk obstetric specialist such as myself.

The couple's first child was going to be born with an open spine defect that would result in lower extremity paralysis as well as bowel and bladder dysfunction. In addition, the spinal defect was creating an abundance of fluid in the brain's ventricles, causing considerable pressure and damage to the brain. If the couple's child survived, it would require numerous complicated operations as well as lifelong care.

Explaining the facts to this understandably alarmed young couple wasn't easy. They, like many of us, were brought up with the notion that they would someday marry, live in a house surrounded by a picket fence, have healthy children, and eventually end up playing with their children's children.

Suddenly, their dreams were shattered and a new reality was creeping in. The world, as this couple knew it, was now totally disrupted. But despite their young age and inexperience, they were somehow going to have to find the strength, courage, and will to carry on—they had no choice.

As I watched their facial expressions and body language during our discussion, I could sense that my patient and her husband were not only feeling helpless and lost, but also baffled. How could this possibly be happening?

I realized that this couple needed support through this difficult time, so I asked them where they found solace in their lives, and to whom they could turn. Unfortunately, they didn't know. They had no such person or place to go for help. Simultaneously, they began to cry.

This tragic scenario is repeated all too often in doctors' offices every day as people are given news that portends serious illness or impending death for themselves or loved ones. How do individuals handle these tragic events? How do they find the resolve to go on?

I have asked many people this question, and I have received an assortment of answers. The vast majority of those who *do* have a source for strength and courage identify their religious institutions and their friends and family members. Reaching out for help can often be the key to opening doors to peace and acceptance.

Yet, these nurturing and comforting support systems often need augmentation in the form of isolated forms of reflection. Long, solitary walks on a beach; hiking into the mountains or through a park; a day spent fly-fishing; sitting alone on a back porch watching the sun go down; jogging on familiar paths; or lying on a blanket in the middle of an open field looking into the heavens, are a few methods that can truly help people gather strength and courage.

It seems to me that, regardless of our age, it is essential that we emotionally and spiritually prepare ourselves for that inevitable moment in our lives when someone will say to us: "I'm sorry to have to tell you this, but . . ."

❧ ❧ ❧

Courage, Faith, and Strong Will

EVERY NOW AND THEN, a patient comes into my obstetric practice who makes me stop and marvel at the courage, faith, and strong will that some human beings are able to display at times of enormous crisis in their lives.

Such a patient (along with her husband) entered my office in 1993.

She was young, married, and four months pregnant. She was being treated for a serious form of cancer and had been sent to me to help determine how to manage this difficult challenge. As I listened to her story, I saw great concern in her eyes. I also noted a pretty smile that seemed to sprinkle hope throughout the room.

This woman had a little girl at home and knew she was to avoid another pregnancy for at least a few years so as not to complicate her treatment plan. But, as so often is the case, this pregnancy "just happened," and she and her husband needed support and guidance.

Tests revealed no obvious signs or symptoms of recurrence of her cancer, yet it had not been long since she finished her chemotherapy, and she was very early in her post-treatment phase. Because of all this, we were not sure of her state of remission.

Tests also revealed a healthy-appearing little boy on ultrasound examination, and the information gathered showed no evidence of fetal injury from previous tests or drugs. The dilemma was straightforward. If this woman maintained the pregnancy, statistics indicated that she ran a higher chance of early recurrence and death. If she ended the pregnancy to save herself, her child would lose its life. Carefully, I attempted to explain all the nuances of such a predicament as my patient and her husband listened intently.

Her response after a few days of deliberation with friends and family was quick and to the point: "Do everything you can to save my baby and me, and I will do everything I can to help you. And Dr. Boehm, one more thing. I have been properly informed of all the bad things that can happen to me and my baby. Now let's put away the bad news and only look at the good."

That was where the courage came in.

The pregnancy was not easy. Weekly visits increasingly revealed evidence of cancer recurrence. Yet, each visit also brought a smile and words to the effect of: "I believe everything will be all right." Finally and inexorably, the tumor reared its ugly head.

Treatment that was delayed to reduce problems for the fetus could no longer be withheld. A plan was devised to limit treatment to her recurrence site. The hope was that this would prolong the critical time needed to help the woman's fetus achieve a more advanced gestational age, and thereby ensure its survival.

"I'll be all right," she told me. "Do it."

That was where the faith came in.

When, at 32 weeks of pregnancy, extensive cancer therapy needed to be implemented, we could wait no longer. I delivered the baby and brought forth into this world a beautiful four-pound healthy little boy. On that day, tears of happiness were shed throughout the room.

We then turned our attention to her second request—to save *her*. Oncologists went to work removing her bone marrow, and then gave her chemotherapeutic drugs that caused baldness, extreme weight loss, and exhaustion—but hopefully, a state of remission. They then returned her bone marrow while keeping close watch over her in an isolated area of the hospital for more than five weeks.

When I visited her room to check on her and talk with her about her pain and loneliness, I was made even more aware of what this woman was still going through.

That was where the strong will came in.

Saving One Life

MY 39-YEAR-OLD PREGNANT PATIENT had just arrived in the emergency room, and I was told that she had suffered a massive intracranial hemorrhage and was comatose. Her only possible chance for survival was emergency brain surgery.

Hurrying down the hall to reach her bedside, I remembered that she was only 24 weeks pregnant, and that the life of her fetus might be in danger as well. As an obstetrician, I do not deal with many dying patients, so it was especially emotional and difficult for me to witness my patient lying in bed unconscious, fighting for her own life and that of her child.

Despite his mother's predicament, however, her six-month old male fetus could be seen with the use of ultrasound technology, swimming around freely in his mother's uterus, mindless of any world but his own.

Watching my patient being wheeled to the operating room, I was already contemplating the events that would unfold after surgery. If the surgery failed, we would be faced with a healthy fetus needing just a little more time before he could be delivered, and a comatose mother needing life support to stay alive long enough to continue to provide a safe environment for her unborn child.

Following the surgery, when my patient failed to come out of her coma, the decision about what to do was made by our medical team—which included dozens of specialists—and my patient's husband.

It was decided that my patient would be kept on life support. For a total of ten weeks, music was played in her room, while family members and health-care providers continually spoke to her as if she was able to hear and understand.

Every attempt was made to keep things as normal as possible for the unborn child, and food given intravenously and life-sustaining oxygen continued to keep my patient alive. All this was done in an effort to allow the fetus to exit his home and enter our normal nursery without complications.

Tests were regularly run to assure the health of the fetus. However, when one such test indicated early fetal distress, a cesarean section was quickly performed, and I delivered a healthy six-pound, four-ounce baby boy.

Later, having never regained consciousness, his mother quietly died.

Because such situations are extremely rare, the medical profession has little experience and understanding of the extremely complex ethical, legal, and social issues surrounding such tragic cases. There are also incredibly high costs involved in such efforts.

Despite the controversy, I know one thing. The day I delivered my comatose patient and held her son in my arms, I was filled with an overwhelming feeling of accomplishment and pride.

All of a sudden, the phrase "life and death" had new meaning.

The Emotional Side of Doctors

I HAVE ALWAYS BEEN EMOTIONAL. As a child, for reasons probably more genetic than anything else (my parents were the same way), I noticed that I felt things more intensely than many of my friends. When my grandfather died, I thought I was going to explode with pain, and when I lost my dog, I was inconsolable.

So I guess I was not surprised that, as a young physician, I frequently found that I was enormously affected by what was happening to my patients. While tears did not always flow, sympathy and empathy certainly did.

I can vividly remember the first time I actually cried in front of a patient's family. I'm glad I did, for I learned a couple of important lessons that day.

As an intern in obstetrics, I often had to help attending physicians care for their private patients. I was 26 years old and full of energy, curiosity, and a desire to learn. A pleasant 30-year-old pregnant woman walked onto our labor-and-delivery floor late one afternoon, complaining of uterine contractions. This was her first pregnancy, and she and her husband were excited about having their first child.

So far, her pregnancy had been uncomplicated and normal. Examining her, however, I noticed that she was bleeding more than usual, so I called her private doctor to fill him in. I told him about her bleeding and that she was contracting quite frequently, without any sign that her uterus was resting between contractions. In fact, her uterus was rigid and tender. He instructed me to start an intravenous drip, cross-match blood, and take her to the operating room where he would meet us. His primary diagnosis was an abruption of her placenta.

An abruption is a serious condition caused when the afterbirth (placenta) is prematurely separated from its attachment to the uterine wall, causing bleeding, fetal distress, and occasionally, maternal distress. Maternal blood loss can be massive, and shock and blood-clotting problems can occur. For the fetus, the condition can be equally serious. The exchange of oxygen between mother and baby can be seriously curtailed, since the placenta is no longer completely attached to the uterus.

I knew all this as I completed my chores, readying our patient for a probable cesarean section. Within approximately 30 minutes, I was fully scrubbed and assisting this woman's private physician as he began to perform an emergency C-section. The family, which included the patient's husband and parents, were directed to the waiting area.

As we opened the uterus, a large amount of bright red blood oozed out, confirming the initial diagnosis of an abruption of the placenta. What followed, however, made my knees weak and my head spin. Quickly delivering the child, it was obvious to us that this otherwise normal-appearing male newborn was dead. Pediatricians who had earlier been called to our operating room were unable to resuscitate this pale and limp baby.

Then, within minutes of the delivery, the anesthesiologist was suddenly moving frantically behind the surgical drapes. When we inquired what was going on, he told us that our patient's blood pressure was dropping and that he was having trouble finding a pulse. Having sustained a life-threatening condition called amniotic fluid embolism, our entire team was now attempting to save this young woman's life. Amniotic fluid embolism is a sudden and massive infusion of amniotic fluid into the mother's circulation, causing a serious allergic reaction.

Despite vigorous cardiopulmonary resuscitation, our attempts failed, and we pronounced our patient dead.

I was reeling. In the space of no more than an hour, we had lost two patients: a mother-to-be and her child.

Unaware of what had just transpired, our patient's family was anxiously awaiting news of the birth of a healthy child and a visit with its new mother.

As I followed the late patient's physician down the hall and into the waiting room, I could feel a lump in my throat. How in the world was this doctor going to tell the family what had just happened to their wife and daughter?

It has been many years since that day, and my memory of the words used to explain what happened is no longer with me. Yet, I clearly remember the stunned expressions and the chaotic disbelief in their eyes.

I could no longer hold back the tears. Noticing my anguish, the patient's mother suddenly came up to me, put her arms around me, and said, "Thank you for caring. I know all of you did what you could."

It was then that I realized that patients and their families care very much how their physicians feel, and that our sentiments impact their attitude toward medical professionals as a whole.

As I retreated to the doctor's lounge, a feeling of helplessness and anguish consumed me. Sitting in the quiet of what I thought was an empty room, I heard the muffled sounds of someone crying. It was the patient's doctor. Believing that no one else was in the room, he had also broken down and was letting his emotions flow.

That day I learned that I was not alone. There would be others who felt as intensely as I did. And those others would be my colleagues.

The Definition of Happiness

WHEN I WAS A CHILD, my mother would often ask me if I was happy. It seemed that if I was happy, she was happy, so I usually answered yes, never really considering what happiness was, or for that matter, if I really was truly happy.

As I grew older, my mother's question changed slightly to "How are you doing?" or "Are you okay?" Yet I knew that my mother was still checking on my state of happiness. Her concern for my well-being never ceased. Her final question of me minutes before she died was that ever-present inquiry, "How are you doing, son?"

Consequently, I have given a lot of thought over the years to the nature of happiness. What was it, how would I achieve it, and was it truly an important goal in life? Thomas Jefferson and his colleagues thought happiness was important, so much so that they included it in the Declaration of Independence, which states that we should be able to enjoy life, liberty, and the pursuit of happiness.

Despite my mother's desire that I always be happy, one thing I learned at a very early age was that I could not be happy all the time. A toast I often hear at weddings confirms that point: "May you have much happiness, and just enough sorrow to know the difference."

Go to your local bookstore and you will find hundreds of books on how to be happy. The Dalai Lama penned a bestseller on this topic, and there is even a perfume on the market called "Happy." Americans are flocking to meditation centers, houses of worship, and even drug dealers to find that ever-elusive feeling of happiness. In some cases, it's working, and in others, it's not.

Interestingly, many Americans do not feel happy. A University of Chicago survey indicates that only three out of ten Americans admit to being happy, and one out of ten actually states that they're unhappy. The remaining six report that they're "pretty happy." Pretty happy . . . what does that mean?

Comedian George Carlin confuses the matter by asking the question, "What does 'more than happy' mean?" Every now and then I find myself telling people I would be more than happy to do this or that. Carlin jokes that "more than happy" sounds like a psychiatric condition. Perhaps he's right.

I may not understand much about the concept of happiness, but one thing I've learned as I've grown older is that inner peace and happiness cannot be bought. While having money can bring comfort and security, it cannot bring about a sense of happiness. I know many people who have few material possessions but who appear very happy, and I know those who are financially secure yet seem quite miserable.

Maybe the definition of happiness is not as difficult as we seem to think it is. Perhaps being happy is knowing that *those you love* are happy. My mother certainly seemed to believe that.

All right. I will give the definition of happiness a shot: Happiness is the feeling I get when I consider how lucky I am to live in a free society; to be healthy, safe, and secure; to live with a woman I love who also loves me; and to have three children who, when I ask them, tell me, "Yes, Dad, we're happy."

God's Cathedral

A 1998 CBS NEWS POLL OF 825 ADULTS revealed some interesting facts about how Americans feel about the effect of prayer on personal health. Eight out of ten surveyed indicated that they believed prayer or other spiritual practices could help speed the recovery of illness, and one out of five was convinced that personal prayer actually cured them.

However, in a *New England Journal of Medicine* article on the subject of religion and medicine, the authors pointed out that while many claimed that religious activities promote health, "the evidence is generally weak and unconvincing, since it is based on studies with serious methodological flaws, conflicting findings, and data that lack clarity and specificity." The authors cautioned physicians not to encourage patients to attend religious services or to engage in other religious activities in an attempt to be healed, and they state that "there is no convincing evidence that religious activities are associated with improved health."

While I tend to believe that the above writers are correct in their scientific evaluation of the subject, I'm also convinced that adding spirituality to one's life can nonetheless have a profound effect on how one handles illness—even if a cure is not necessarily effected. It can significantly enhance one's feelings of self and purpose, help to bring about a sense of inner peace and tranquility, create a feeling of oneness with the world, and generate a better understanding of the meaning of life. The beneficial results of spirituality in our lives allow for a better handling of our afflictions, our pain, and our sorrow.

It is this spirituality that so many Americans seek yet often have difficulty finding. With our society focusing on materialism, superficiality, efficiency, and productivity, it's not surprising that so many Americans feel an emptiness and a longing for purpose. Americans have come to understand that money cannot buy a feeling of meaning in their lives, and that something less tangible and more spiritual is required.

For many, spirituality can best be achieved through frequent visitation to houses of worship. Clearly that works for many, but for others this is not the answer to their quest for spiritual infusion.

After spending time hiking in the Canadian Rockies recently, I believe that I have come up with an answer for this latter group, as well as a recommendation to all those wishing to add a new dimension to their inner faith. It is simply this: Every so often, spend some time in the largest of God's houses of worship—the outdoors—and if possible, take a trip to some of our magnificent national parks.

Leaving behind our busy life, my wife, Julie, and I hiked up and down the tall, majestic mountains of the Rockies for six days. I witnessed God's handiwork in the beauty of turquoise-colored Moraine Lake, which was surrounded by snow-capped mountain peaks and meadows covered with intensely colored wildflowers. I could feel God's presence as I stood alone among His towering trees and rolling hills, and I could hear Him in the absence of all sound, save that of the wind as it moved across the meadow.

Everywhere I went and everything I gazed upon brought forth the feeling of God's grandeur, of my personal insignificance, and of my incredible fortune to be a part of His design.

I decided to augment and reinforce those feelings upon my return home by visiting the smaller chapels of nature in our city, and I hope to someday return to the larger cathedrals that God has provided for us humans as a reminder of all that is possible.

Thus, when my time comes to deal with any physical afflictions, I will have with me what the medical profession cannot and probably will never be able to prove, but that which the majority of us overwhelmingly believe: a spiritual foundation, which will be always be by my side bringing me strength, comfort, and, who knows, perhaps even a cure.

❧ ❧ ❧

Humor and Your Health

IT HAS BEEN SAID THAT DYING is like taking a final exam: You must be prepared. But how does one prepare for such a final life-ending event? This past year, a friend helped me answer that question.

The news of his diagnosis shocked me—he had a malignant tumor and would need surgery. After having a large portion of the right side of his brain removed, Noah was finally able to receive visitors. I was told that his progress was guarded, and that following surgery he had suffered a number of very serious setbacks that required a prolonged stay in the intensive-care unit. His devoted family and friends feared the worst but hoped for the best.

Noah was asleep as I entered his hospital room. His shaved head, obvious scalp incision, and loss of weight were clear signs that a major insult had occurred to this otherwise strong-willed, humorous, opinionated, community-minded business and family man.

His ever-present wife greeted me warmly as I quietly joined her on a nearby sofa. Her radiant smile bathed over me as I listened to her tale of the past two weeks. There were times that it was touch-and-go, she explained, but now Noah was better, and plans for radiation treatments were being made.

Suddenly, my friend opened his eyes and saw me sitting across the room, and he slowly began to speak. His words were barely audible, and I was worried. After having so much of his brain removed, would he be coherent, able to express himself, or even know who I was?

"Hi, Frank," he said. "I'm glad you came."

"So am I," I faintly uttered. Reassured that he knew my name, I continued to listen.

"You know, Frank, all this has taught me a very important lesson. I've learned that money is not everything." He paused, and I thought to myself that my friend was about to espouse an important lesson of life, one that I had heard many times before and one that dealt with the fact that in reality, *health* was everything. I was relieved that my friend's surgery had not left him unable to think logically or philosophically.

"No, Frank," he continued, "money is not everything. Health is 5 percent."

There it was: a joke. It came out of left field. His wife and I began to chuckle, and upon realizing how funny that statement was, we broke into full laughter. Obviously when neurosurgeons removed a portion of my friend's brain, they did not remove the part that controlled his sense of humor. Thank goodness for that.

Ever since I can remember, Noah has always had a joke for me when we've gotten together. Consequently, I always looked forward to seeing him at parties, where he would share his levity with me and others. And now, with his life in the balance, it was humor that he would use to help him prepare for the difficult road that lay ahead. With a twinkle in his eye, he began to spout more one-liners that day at the hospital, and I found myself spending a very enjoyable hour with him and his wife.

Noah continued to bring humor into his life. Although I am sure he addressed the seriousness of his situation, he continued to live life as he always had—to its fullest each day.

Not long after his surgery, he traveled to and participated in the Democratic National Convention in Los Angeles, and began making plans with his wife to remodel their home. And throughout his chemotherapy and radiation treatment, his humor continued to sustain him.

We love to laugh, for it makes us feel good. It relaxes us, releases tension, and improves our overall mood. Good humor, like the kind Noah used that day with his wife and me, revealed his understanding of that concept.

A man who can face adversity with humor is definitely someone who is more than prepared for that final exam.

~ PART II

Special Moments

Special moments are a part of all of our lives now and then, and physicians are no different from anyone else when it comes to partaking of them. In fact, because our profession puts us in daily contact with people at the best and worst of times, we are often privy to extraordinarily moving experiences that can alter us forever.

I have had many special moments, both professionally and personally, which have now become fond memories for me.

No Video Camera Needed

EVERYWHERE I GO, I SEE PEOPLE with video cameras in hand, aiming at their surroundings in an attempt, I suppose, to permanently capture the moment.

For the record, I will admit that I do not own such a camera. It's not that I have anything against modern technology; rather, it's because I believe that I already possess the best video camera there is: my eyes and my brain. After all, that's usually the only "camera" available when special moments occur.

For example, it's the eyes that capture that look of joy on your child's face when she's dancing spontaneously and rhythmically to music. Or maybe it's that last embrace with a loved one that brought tears to your eyes and a conscious, intense desire to remember all the vivid details of that moment.

I have, for example, a wonderful "tape" of a very special moment in my life. Eyes open or shut, I see it in color. I need no machine to help me play it back, and no special room to view it.

It was to be my father's last winter in Florida, the place he loved more than anywhere else. He and I had a special, loving relationship, so my visit to Fort Lauderdale during the winter holidays invariably brought us considerable joy. As always, I called him from my wife's family home nearby as soon as I arrived, and we agreed to meet on the beach. Being two miles apart, I was to jog south toward his home, while he would begin walking north to meet me somewhere in the middle.

As I slowly jogged past the multitude of sun worshipers and bathers, I listened to the waves and wind as well as the beautiful, mellow music piped into my ears by a small radio attached to my waist. With the sun beating down its warm, welcoming rays, I was enjoying the feeling of the sand beneath my feet and, and most of all, anticipating the reunion with my dad. I was filled with happiness.

I saw him appear in the distance. His gait, so similar to mine, was unmistakable, and assured me that it was indeed my father who was approaching me on that sunny day on the beach in Lauderdale by the Sea.

And then something wonderful happened. Unable to run because of his age, he nonetheless stretched out his arms as if to embrace me, and with quicker steps than usual, pointedly made his way toward me, all the while glowing with his familiar and reassuring smile. In like manner, I stretched out my arms; and while covering the next 50 yards or so with the wind at my back, the sun in my face, and the music in my ears, I ran toward him.

My heart seemed to burst with joy. I could feel moisture in my eyes as I reached his outstretched arms, and we embraced and held each other tight. No words were spoken—there was just the sensation of our beating hearts and our swollen pride.

Suddenly, we heard applause. Other people along the beach—many my father's age—witnessed this delicious moment between father and son, and felt as moved as we did. We laughed, and arm-in-arm, walked to meet my mother, who eagerly awaited us.

❖ ❖ ❖

Being trained as a physician, I am perhaps more attuned to my surroundings and aware of the body language of those I interface with, but we all have the ability to turn on our own "video camera" at those special moments. We just need prac-tice, and the willingness to use it.

That special moment on the beach on that sunny winter day with all its vivid details is permanently imbedded in my mind. It can never be erased until I—as my beloved father did that next fall—pass away.

Thank God I had my camera with me that day.

A Dad's Rite of Passage

ON THE SURFACE, it was just like any other hot August day in Nashville. But for me, it was a day filled with roller coaster-like emotions—ranging from the high surrounding my 18-year-old son's departure for college, to a mid-level wash of nostalgia and memories, and finally, to a low filled with sadness and emptiness.

This particular morning, my son Todd was very much on my mind as I arose early to help him get packed. I was not expecting this to be an overly emotional day, yet memories overwhelmed me. I remembered the first day his mother and I dropped him off at kindergarten, and how we felt so uneasy—overly concerned and sad. I remembered his Bar Mitzvah, when he stood before his family and friends at the tender age of 13 and recited his portion of our Holy Scripture with perfection, thereby entering Jewish adulthood. Then, too, I noted a lump in my throat and a tug at my heart.

I remembered the times we spent alone and the times we shared with the rest of the family, and I felt a great deal of pride. Todd was my quiet, gentle, sensitive, skeptical, shy, and intelligent computer-wizard son. He had managed to cope with his mother's departure from our lives when he was ten years old, and despite his shyness and lack of athletic prowess, he had survived the rigors of adolescence.

My memories in check somewhat, I now knew that it was time to go. The car was packed, and Todd was ready. It was I who lingered and procrastinated. I wanted to have one more conversation with my son, one more attempt to tell him all he would ever need to know about life in the real world.

I wanted to prepare him for college life, to help him avoid the mistakes I had made at that time in my life. But as I sat on the edge of his bed that afternoon in August, I couldn't speak. Instead, I cried.

My understanding son sat quietly, knowing that he could do nothing, and patiently waited until I finished. Finally, I said I was ready, and without saying another word, we left our home and got into the car.

Now, lest you think I was sending my son off on a plane clear across the country, or even driving him to a destination hours away from home, I was not. I was merely driving him to his dormitory, which was six miles from my home and less than 100 yards from my office at the medical center. You see, I was taking my son to Vanderbilt University to begin the first four years of his college education.

Driving home alone that evening in a pensive mood, I remembered friends who had told me how they felt when they took their children to school or sent them off for four weeks of summer camp for the first time. Their feelings were similar to the ones I had on that day, so I wondered if it really was just the separation from our children that brought forth so many heartfelt emotions, or if it was something else.

After thinking about it, I realized that my feelings had little to do with my son and everything to do with *me*. I was not afraid for him; I was afraid for *myself*. It was a rite of passage for me—a time to end one segment of my life and move on to another.

My son's departure for college, and all those other periods of transition that we parents have to deal with, symbolize an end of a stage of life that is well known and comfortable, to one that is unknown and somewhat frightening. How would I spend my day when there were no children to cook for and feed, to entertain or teach? What or who would take their place in my life?

Did all this really mean that I was getting old and wouldn't have much use anymore? No. Todd had a younger brother, Tommy; and a sister, Catherine, so I wouldn't be so lonely after all, and my life really wouldn't change that much.

I knew I would go through this whole scenario again when Tommy departed the following autumn. Only next year, I would handle it all a little better, and be able to acknowledge that Tommy, and eventually Catherine, would leave and never really return—except for occasional trips home for holidays and the like—and that they and I would be better for it. Fortunately, we humans are adaptable, as we are always changing and growing.

That's really what life is all about, isn't it?

Awe and Wonder

LIKE MOST PROFESSIONS, medicine has its boring and mundane moments. However, there have been many times when being a physician has instilled me with awe and wonder.

One of those instances occurred five years ago when I was called to the hospital's labor-and-delivery suite to take care of a patient carrying quintuplets. Although only 24 weeks pregnant, my patient was in premature labor. Despite vigorous attempts to stop her progress, she was about to bring five new human beings into this world.

As we wheeled her into the delivery room, we all knew that trouble lay ahead. These five babies were four months premature and only had a one-in-five chance of survival. If they survived, each child would need intensive care for an extended period of time in our newborn nursery.

Within minutes, I was standing in place, ready to deliver the first quintuplet. Gazing around, I noticed the enormous amount of equipment and personnel in the delivery room. Standing by the resuscitation tables were several medical professionals, each waiting their turn to receive one of the quintuplets. A certain amount of apprehension could be seen on their faces.

At the head of the patient's table were three anesthesia personnel prepared to do what was needed to bring this new litter of children into the world. There were also two obstetric nurses readying the room for our big event, and standing with me were three obstetric residents.

One resident was constantly monitoring the small and fragile babies in the uterus with an ultrasound machine, while the other two stood fully scrubbed, ready to assist me. Standing in the corner were two medical students, absolutely amazed by what they were about to witness. Finally, sitting quietly next to his wife, was the father-to-be, staring with disbelief at this spectacle he had helped create.

One at a time, the babies began their journey down the birth canal. Head first, Stephen appeared, followed by his siblings Stephanie, Clinton, Barbara, and Christopher. As each baby fell into my waiting arms, I carefully cut the umbilical cord and handed the child to a waiting pediatric team member.

Finally, it was over. What seemed like an hour was in reality only a few minutes. I had just delivered five tiny human beings into this world, and I was truly filled with awe and wonder. Although every birth can easily be described as awe-inspiring, after delivering more than 10,000 babies in my lifetime, I admit that many feel quite routine. But not this time. While I had delivered many twins and perhaps a dozen triplets in my career, I had never delivered quintuplets. Since spontaneous occurrence of quintuplets is approximately one in 15 million pregnancies, it is an extraordinarily rare and unique event. But the human uterus is made for only one child at a time, and multiple births cause problems for both mother and babies.

In this case, our excitement was soon followed by disappointment and sorrow as we helplessly watched Stephanie, Clinton, Barbara, and Christopher lose their fight for life.

❧ ❧ ❧

What I felt that night years ago went beyond mere awe and wonder. It included humility. Being a part of such an incredible miracle of nature can easily bring forth such a feeling. How small and insignificant we humans are in comparison to the miracle of birth and death.

Not long ago, the one surviving child, Stephen, a healthy, happy and loving boy, rushed into my arms when he saw me at the hospital. The feeling of humility quickly returned—as well as the awe and wonder I feel when I realize how fortunate I am to be part of this magnificent profession—and this wonderful world.

❧ ❧ ❧

The Healing Powers of Joy

MEDICAL BOOKS ARE FILLED with descriptions of medications for the heart. From the well-known drug digitalis, to newer types of pharmaceuticals that stimulate heart muscles, dilate coronary vessels, or block harmful arrhythmias, there seems to be no shortage of effective medicines for people with heart ailments.

There is, however, a "medicine" for the human heart that is not found in medical textbooks or recommended by health-care professionals. It has the potential and capacity to stimulate an aching heart, rush additional oxygen-enriched blood to all parts of the body, inspire feelings of intense pride, and cause a swelling sensation in the chest.

That medicine is called *joy*—and during the summer of 1993, I took a dose of it myself.

❖ ❖ ❖

A typical Middle Eastern cloudless blue sky covered our small group of family and friends as we gathered on Mt. Scopus overlooking the city of Jerusalem to celebrate my daughter's Bat Mitzvah.

Literally meaning "daughter of the commandment," a Bat Mitzvah is a Jewish tradition for 13-year-old girls (boys get a Bar Mitzvah). A Bat Mitzvah occurs after many years of religious study culminating in a religious service where the teenager reads from the sacred Torah (the Hebrew version of the first five books of the Bible). The ceremony, considered a milestone in the life of a Jewish girl, marks her entry into religious adulthood.

Catherine had worked very hard to achieve this goal, one that her father, brothers, grandfathers, and great-grandfathers had also experienced at 13 years of age. Standing at this historic landmark in Israel, I could feel the warm rays of the sun shining down on my face as I watched my daughter perform her duties with poise, expertise, and maturity. I was filled with an enormous sense of pride, love, and joy.

Anyone who has ever witnessed such an event as I did that beautiful August day knows how I felt. It's similar to what one feels during any of life's precious moments, such as births, graduations, weddings, anniversaries, and birthdays. These occasions can fill us with such profound pleasure that it's almost as if we've just been given a potent medicine.

Joy is a medication that improves circulation, while also creating intense euphoria and peace. I don't have a heart condition; however, I'm sure that the joy I experienced on that special day as I watched my daughter perform a ritual passed down from generation to generation, made my heart stronger and healthier.

I am convinced that all of us should medicate ourselves with joy as often as possible.

The Fringe Benefits of Being a Physician

DOCTORS LIVE IN A WORLD that combines both the joy and pain of life's precious and significant moments. While many working people consider their jobs less than satisfying, physicians often express sincere pleasure when discussing their work.

This is true for me as well. However, I must admit that there have been times when it's been two in the morning, a delivery isn't going smoothly, and I'm picturing an office full of patients the next morning—and I've felt less than overjoyed.

Yet, there's also that moment when I'm about to deliver a baby, with an expectant mother pushing so hard that her neck veins appear close to rupture—and her husband is sitting by her side looking on with amazement and apprehension. The obstetric nurse is scurrying around the three of us as I lift a wet, screaming baby from beneath draped legs and exclaim, "It's a boy!" Then I know that it's all been worth it. I can always sleep later.

How many professions have that as a fringe benefit?

There are other advantages, too. For example, doctors are often the first to admit that while it is our role and duty to teach our patients, it is often our *patients* who teach us the most valuable lessons of life. One of those lessons particularly stands out.

I was in Southern California studying at the City of Hope Medical Center. I was 29 years old, finishing my OB-GYN training, and was now taking time out to concentrate on the art and science of cancer surgery. My responsibilities included working in a breast cancer clinic. There I would see approximately 20 patients every Wednesday afternoon, most of whom had advanced forms of the disease and who were returning weekly to receive their chemotherapy treatment.

It was during one of these clinics, while going from room to room, that I sat down to speak with a middle-aged woman who had metastatic breast cancer. The tumor had spread to her lungs, making it difficult for her to speak. Words came slowly and with great effort, and while we had spoken before on other visits, our times together had been perfunctory and businesslike.

As we sat together in that small examining room, I sat back in my chair, and speaking softly, inquired as to how she was doing. Her response still rings in my mind today. She exclaimed with a smile, "Wonderful!"

Somewhat taken aback, I remarked how interesting it was that she could be so cheerful during such a trying time.

She replied, "The best thing that ever happened to me, Dr. Boehm, was the day I was told I had cancer."

"How could that be?" I asked.

She explained, "Well, before I knew I had cancer, I never really saw the sun set; I was never aware of all the incredible things that life had to offer. But since that day, knowing that each day is limited, and therefore precious, I began to notice the sunset and the sunrise. I heard sounds I never heard before. I smelled fragrances, tasted food, and touched textures as never before. All at once I became alive, and a richness filled my every day."

With eyes slightly moist, I finished my exam and treatment. As I turned to leave, she added, "Just think, Doctor—you could start all that today—*without* cancer."

Three weeks later, she took her last breath and died peacefully in her hospital bed. When I pulled the sheet over her placid face, I knew that a great lesson had been given to me. I would not forget it.

❧ ❧ ❧

Happiness for a Healthy Heart

MY FAMILY HISTORY IS FRAUGHT with heart disease, so I've made a concerted effort to eat properly; exercise regularly; and take vitamins, a daily baby aspirin, and a cholesterol-lowering drug each day. I also have an annual physical exam to make sure that my heart is healthy and strong.

But, as I've said previously, I believe that happiness plays an important role as a preventive health measure. I've encouraged my patients to fill their lives with as much joy as possible, because a happy heart is also a strong heart, and can better handle the stresses that we all encounter from time to time throughout our lives.

There may be some who doubt that happiness can really affect the health of a vital, muscular organ such as the heart, since there is no medical research data to prove such a concept. But as I see it, although hard evidence is lacking, an injection of joy in one's life certainly can't hurt!

This past summer, I had the opportunity to fill my heart with happiness at my son's wedding. As I watched my first-born take his vows, I could not help but remember everything we had shared since his entry into the world (and into my arms) 29 years ago in that small delivery room in New Haven Community Hospital.

I remembered his first words, those unsteady early steps, his spontaneous smile, and his passages in and out of the various stages of growth and development. From his first day at nursery school to this day standing at the altar, memories flooded back to me.

I remembered the good times, as well as the trials and tribulations we had endured together. I recalled every stage of raising and nurturing him, until the day he left home to start college.

As Todd stood hand-in-hand with his soon-to-be wife, Jennifer, I knew that he was embarking on his greatest life cycle. He was about to join forces with another in life's toils and pleasures. Hopefully, they would also join together in the reproductive process. I smiled as I considered the prospect. Perhaps I would become a grandparent someday and experience even greater jubilation.

My feelings soared as I looked around the room at family and friends who had gathered for this festive occasion. I'm sure it cleansed and opened my arteries, improved my circulation, and strengthened my cardiac muscle. I know that the pride and love I felt must have had an extremely positive effect on this most vital of all human organs.

I believe that we should all make a resolution to seek out ways to bring happiness into our lives as often as possible, because, as the saying goes, while happiness may not add years to our life, it can certainly add life to our years.

Thank You, David

LIFE IS OFTEN FILLED WITH REGRETS. While some of those regrets are trivial in nature and bear little impact on our lives, there are others that are more significant in terms of how we view ourselves. There is much validity to that old axiom that we are the sum total of our experiences.

I came to realize the truth of this even more clearly last Thanksgiving. I was seated in the aisle seat in the third row of a Southwest Airlines flight to Florida. Sitting by the window was a cute little boy, who was, as I was later to learn, six years old and on his way to visit his father for the holiday.

We started to chat, and there was instant chemistry between the two of us. Little David quickly called me Frankie and began to talk, play, cajole, and show me his wonderful and charming personality. Suddenly the paperwork in front of me did not seem so important, and the work I had planned to do during the flight was put away under my seat.

I was hooked. This child was one of those special little kids whom you do not often get a chance to meet. I did not want to miss out on this opportunity.

David told me about himself in his six-year-old style of speaking. He was really excited about going to see his father—no doubt about it, he was going to push his dad into the swimming pool before he returned home at the end of the weekend. I also learned that David was an only child. This sounded very familiar . . . so was I. He smiled when I shared this fact with him.

David drew pictures for me, smiling with pride as he finished each one. I taught him a game I had long ago taught my three children, but hadn't played for over a decade. Without doing anything more than explaining the rules one time, David beat me handily—and twice at that. David told me that he played that king of all games, chess, so we talked about different moves.

Clearly, I thought to myself on the bumpy ride down south, *this is one of those kids who is smart, cute, personable, and warm, and who will probably be just like that when he grows up.*

Walking off the plane together, along with the flight attendant, David and I said our good-byes. As quickly as the little guy had entered my life, he was gone.

Over the course of the next few days, I began to wonder why this chance meeting and encounter with a young boy named David continued to capture my interest, attention, and emotions so much.

At first glance, it seemed obvious. I missed those times when my children were his age, and I needed a "fix." David reminded me of the precious moments I'd spent with my kids when they were growing up.

However, upon further reflection, my memories also inspired regrets. Those days are somewhat blurred for me now, but I probably didn't spend as much time with my children as I should have. I was working hard building my career, and there were times when I was just too tired to play with them or give them the attention they craved.

As I look back, I wish I had known then what I know now. Those early years with our children come and go so swiftly that we have to grab every moment we can before they pass.

By interacting with David, my regrets were softened, though. For a few hours, I was given a glimpse back, and was reminded of all those wonderful times that I *did* share with my children.

Thanks, David, wherever you are.

The Way We Were

AN INVITATION TO MY 40TH HIGH SCHOOL REUNION had been on my desk for a while, and I kept asking myself, *Am I going, and if so, why?*

I had been to other reunions, and although they were enjoyable, afterwards I usually told myself that I would probably never attend one again. But it had been a long time since my last reunion, so I thought, *Well, maybe I'll go one more time.*

But why? After all, I really hadn't kept in touch with many of my 1958 classmates since we'd graduated. While I did have a few lifelong buddies from back then, I really didn't need to go to a reunion to be with them—since I saw them anyway.

I kept thinking that there must be a good reason why I was considering attending. If I went, I would want my wife to accompany me, although it probably wouldn't be that interesting for her. After all, this was *my* reunion, not hers. Yet, if I did go, I would still want her to be with me because I'm proud of her and want to show her off. To be honest, I'd also want to let everyone know what *I've* accomplished. Okay, maybe that's why I was thinking of going—I just wanted to show off.

But no, when I gave it additional thought, I realized that that wasn't really the case either. I knew that I was a lot older and wiser now than I was back then, and I'd stopped caring so much about what others thought of me.

I looked in the mirror for an answer. Everyone says that I "look good," yet I learned from my father years ago that life is divided into three stages: youth, middle age, and "you're looking good." So that's not really much of a compliment anymore.

I paged through my old high school yearbook for answers, and thought, *Maybe that's why I want to go, to see how my classmates have aged. Will I be able to recognize them from their old photos, or will I have to quickly glance at their name tags? But why should I care how they look? I know that we've all aged.*

If it wasn't to see old friends, show off, or compare how I'd aged with others, then what exactly was the reason I would want to attend my 40th high school reunion?

Suddenly it hit me. I wanted to go back to a very special time. The present and future consume so much of my life that I was looking forward to spending at least a few days in the past. And what a past those high school days had been.

It was during those crucial four years that I traversed puberty and adolescence and reached adulthood. It was then that I started formulating the ideas that led to important decisions about my future.

Like many of us, my time in high school was filled with successes, failures, anxiety, excitement, insecurity, learning, laughter, and fun. So, while many who shared those years with me are no longer a part of my life, I wanted to once again be in their presence and say thanks for sharing four very important years of my life with me.

That's a great reason for going to a reunion . . . and I realized that I couldn't wait to go.

Happy Birthday, Dad!

THE DAY OF ONE'S BIRTH is an important date. Not only does it mark the beginning of life's inevitable countdown, but it's also an annual reminder of our resiliency and vulnerability.

For this and a host of other reasons, I truly enjoy celebrating my own birthday, as well as that of my loved ones. Part of my love for this special day stems from the fact that my parents made birthdays so meaningful. From the moment I woke up on the morning of my birthday, to the minute I went to sleep, my birthdays were filled with wonderful gifts; expressions of love, fun, and frivolity; and a heightened awareness of how precious we all were to each other.

When one of my parents was celebrating their own birthday, I remember well the cards carefully signed the night before, the pride I felt when I handed my parents yet another object I had made especially for them, and the shower of hugs and kisses that was bestowed on me as a result. I also vividly remember the special events that filled the day, and the clinking of glasses as toasts were made later in the evening.

I'm sure that these memories explain why, despite my parents' deaths, I still have poignant and unique feelings on their birthdays. Each year since they've passed away, on the day of their birth, I have quietly and privately celebrated those once-upon-a-time joyous occasions.

Had he still been alive, March 4 would have been my father's 95th birthday. Although he's been dead more than ten years, he still lives on in my mind. While I admit that there are days when I don't think of him, there are many more days when he is constantly in my thoughts.

However, my father was very much on my mind on that one particular 4th day of March when I rose earlier than usual to attend to a woman who was about to deliver her first child. After many years of a childless marriage, followed by a complicated and difficult pregnancy, my patient finally brought a beautiful six-pound baby girl into the world. You could feel the joy in the air and see the tears falling. But not all the tears that were shed that day came from my patient's eyes.

Holding this very special and precious bundle in my arms, I hesitated before routinely handing this little girl to her anxiously waiting parents. The symbolism that existed for me in that moment was indescribably intense. I felt that this baby's birth was a wonderfully significant celebration of my father's life—a man who would always mean the world to me.

And so as I drove home that morning of my father's birthday, I felt that *this* year I had celebrated his birthday in an especially unique and marvelous way. I had helped bring life into the world and had witnessed the ultimate joy experienced by new parents.

For me, a circle had been completed. Because my father had sacrificed so much so that I could enter the field of medicine, I was able to be a part of this blessed event. I celebrated the birth of the little baby I had just delivered, and I also celebrated the life of a parent who would always live on in my heart.

Happy Birthday, Dad!

Family Values

POLITICIANS ARE TALKING A LOT THESE DAYS about family values; however, as far as I'm concerned, it's mostly talk.

I've actually come up with an idea myself for people who want to bring the family unit closer together and avoid so many of the social problems confronting us. While there may be many ways to instill important values in our children, one excellent way is to take a family vacation.

While I was growing up, my parents took me on a vacation to South Florida each summer. The four days we spent driving to and from our destination, in addition to ten fun-filled days together in the sun, represented the most memorable and enjoyable part of my year. Our family vacation allowed us to really connect with each other—far away from the hustle and bustle of everyday life.

I looked forward to those two weeks with such anticipation that sleep the night before we left was nearly impossible. Except for our annual two-week vacation, my dad worked six days a week as a salesman in a men's clothing store and usually came home late, so our time together was limited. However, from the moment we left home for our trip, we were together 24 hours a day.

During these trips, my dad held my little hand as we walked on the beach and held me in his arms as we ran into the ocean. My parents and I had time to get to know each other better because we were able to appreciate our quality time together.

We also took lots of pictures. Most of these snapshots are now in albums stored away, but many are still quite vivid in my mind. To this day, these memories still instill a feeling of peace and tranquility in me.

My father and mother did a lot more for me during those two weeks each summer than they probably ever realized. Although we had very little money, they made every effort to make sure that I was happy and having fun. Even those times that were not so happy and not so much fun were still times that we spent *together,* sharing whatever was happening at the moment.

Going back to the issue of family values, I realize that it was on that two-week vacation each year that one of the most important family values was developed and reinforced in me—the feeling of belonging. Make no mistake about it— feeling like one is a part of something is critical to one's perception of self.

The children who are randomly killing other children in our schools today are often portrayed as loners—isolated kids who don't feel included. Add a little love to that feeling of inclusion—and bingo, you've got real family values.

So, just as my parents treated me, I treated my own children. Although I didn't always have time for a two-week summer vacation . . . sometimes a Saturday-morning walk, a Sunday-afternoon drive, or even a few days out of town accomplished the same goal.

Our children need to feel a sense of inclusion, of togetherness, so they truly know they are a part of something bigger than themselves. That something is called a *family.*

Spring Vacation

As I write this piece, I am on a cruise ship gazing at the Caribbean sunset. My wife, Julie, and I are here to chaperone our daughter and four of her 12th-grade friends while they're on their spring break. But as I watch the sun sink below the horizon, I am again reminded of how much our lives change with every sunrise and sunset.

The ship is huge—it has 2,500 passengers—and there is much to do. For four days, Julie and I will try to stay out of the girls' way, yet at the same time make sure that they're safe. It's an enjoyable assignment—but a little nerve-racking as well.

Although they're 18 years old and quite grown up, these young women still seem like kids to me. I'm filled with a mixture of pride and apprehension as I watch young men congregate around their deck chairs in the afternoon sun. And I smile nervously as I watch my daughter and her friends catch a trolley ride to town for a few hours of shopping, leaving Julie and me behind to wonder whether they will make it back to the ship on time.

This vacation seems different from the many others that I have taken with my little girl—I realize that Catherine has grown up and doesn't really need me to take her on vacations anymore. She no longer needs me to help her build sand castles on the beach or to sit by her side as she hurls through space on a roller coaster. No longer do I need to watch over her, to monitor what she eats or how long she sleeps. My 18-year-old is a senior in high school, ready to go to college, and she's now quite capable of handling these and many more responsibilities on her own.

Watching our children grow up is never easy. We agonize during every significant milestone: when we anxiously leave them with their teacher on their first day of school, when we give them the keys to the car, or when we send them off to college. Each of these moments changes our life permanently.

Having watched two sons leave home, I thought I would be ready this time. However, I don't think that parents are ever really prepared to see their children turn into adults. As I watch Catherine and her friends interact with other teenagers aboard ship and take responsibility for their own vacation activities, I'm proud of her, but I'm also a little saddened to lose my little girl.

In my heart, while I may not be needed on vacations any longer (except financially, of course), I know that Julie and I have helped bring Catherine to a place she can call her own. She is ready for her life away from home. Deep down, I'm aware that even if my little girl doesn't really need me to take care of every little thing on a day-to-day basis, she knows I will always be there for her. No matter how far away she is or how difficult the storms of life may be, my daughter will always feel my presence by her side.

So, as I watch the sun rapidly disappear on the horizon and await our evening meal together, I'm reminded that our lives are in a constant state of change, and like the transition from dawn to dusk, this is what life is all about. For without change, there can be no growth; and without growth, there can be no meaning in life.

A Grandfather's Love

SOMETHING VERY SPECIAL happened to me a few weeks ago. I became a grandfather.

I know that becoming a grandfather is not that unusual . . . but this was my first grandchild!

My son Todd and his wife, Jennifer, brought little Riley Isabel into the world at Atlanta's Northside Hospital, while Julie and I sat in the waiting room. We had been looking forward to this moment for quite some time, but we weren't sure how we'd feel. Everyone kept telling me, "Just wait, you're going to love being a grandfather." But I really couldn't imagine what the reality of the situation would be like.

"You'll just have to sit in the waiting room!" Jennifer's nurse firmly told me as I tried to explain who I was. She wasn't impressed. Despite having delivered thousands of babies, I was suddenly treated like everyone else when it came to the birth of my granddaughter.

While waiting for my son to come get us and show us his new bundle of joy, my thoughts drifted back to a distant time—to my own grandfather.

Opa (German for "grandfather"), as I called him, never learned to speak English, so I learned to speak and understand the German language at a very early age. Immigrating to America in 1939 in order to escape Nazi Germany, my grandparents lived with us in a small three-bedroom flat.

Opa wore three-piece suits with a gold pocket watch, smelled of "4711" cologne, smoked delicious-smelling cigars, and told wonderful stories of his life back in Germany. He took me on walks in the park and around our neighborhood, tightly clutching my hand the entire way as if to ensure that nothing bad would happen to me. I knew he loved me. I could *feel* it. In return, I loved him immensely.

When he died just before my 13th birthday, I was crushed. This proud, elderly, old-world gentleman who held my hand, told me stories, kissed my cheeks, and watched over me, was now gone.

It occurred to me that this same loving bond between my grandfather and me also existed between my son, Todd, and *his* Opa—my dad. That close tie was an important factor in helping my son traverse the trials and tribulations of adolescence. For two summers, he lived with his Opa, and their connection grew even stronger.

Each time my father spoke to me about Todd, his face would light up, and a rim of moisture would fill his eyes. They were very close.

It wasn't until my father died that my son experienced his first loss. I knew as I watched him symbolically shovel dirt onto his Opa's grave at the funeral that my son had been blessed to have such a loving, nurturing, and supportive relationship with my father. . . .

My thoughts were suddenly interrupted by my son's voice: "Come meet Riley Isabel!" he exclaimed as he entered the waiting room. The smile on his face was as large as I had ever witnessed. I waited my turn to hold my little granddaughter, and when I finally had her in my arms, I was overwhelmed with emotion and pride. I was also filled with a feeling of hope—hope that this little girl nestled in my arms would someday feel about me as my son and I had felt about our respective grandfathers.

"I want her to call you Opa," my son said as he looked me in the eyes from across the large labor-and-delivery room. I felt the sting of tears . . . amazing—it was now *my* turn to be Opa.

The genetic composition of this adorable newborn child contained, in part, the DNA of three Opas, along with my son. Riley Isabel was an extension of all of us. She was a link to the past and the future, and a bridge between the generations.

Suddenly, the answer to the question of how it felt to be a grandfather became very clear. I felt extended!

Diary Entry: August 21, 1999

DEAR DIARY,

It is 5:00 a.m., and despite being Saturday morning, I'm awake. As I open my eyes, I know that this is going to be one of those milestone days. Catherine is leaving for college.

I begin my usual morning routine by making coffee and waiting for the newspaper. Since the paper has not yet come, I sit at my desk and do what I often do when I have time on my hands . . . write.

Catherine is my baby, so I know that today will be difficult. She is the last of my children to leave the nest. The other two moved out several years before. It is never easy when our children go off to college. It's not like sending them to camp or on a long vacation. This time they pack all their belongings and make a new home for themselves. Oh, they may come home every so often, but it's mostly for a quick visit—a time to do laundry, rest up, see friends, share meals, tell stories, and then leave once again.

It is now 5:45 A.M., time to wake up Catherine, so I put my pen down and slowly make my way to her bedroom. I sit quietly on the side of her bed and watch her sleep. Once a tiny form to be awakened for another day of play is now a young lady curled up with her pillow. I scratch her back like I always do to wake her. She stirs and opens her eyes. She smiles, remembering what day this is. Memories begin to flood over me. I feel a lump in my throat, so I go downstairs.

"I need to get some gas, Dad," she tells me as she comes down the stairs, dressed and ready to go. I want to spend each remaining moment with her before she leaves, so I go along. We return home and finish packing the little odds and ends that she wants to take with her. Then it's time to go.

Catherine and I have been separated many times since her birth, so this should be no different from all those other times we have said good-bye. Catherine lived in a different city, with only alternate-weekend visits to see me from ages five to ten. And even during the last three years when she has lived with me and Julie, she was always so independent—knowing what she wanted, going here and there, spending summers at camp or traveling. It seemed that we were always saying good-bye. Yet, this time it *does* feel very different, and I wonder why.

My two older sons lived with me until they left for college. I can vividly remember that feeling of uneasiness and melancholy as we said our good-byes. Perhaps because Catherine and I had spent so much time apart over the years and had endured so many good-byes, I believed that this would be different. It isn't. My despondency is once again palpable.

Catherine and I hug in the kitchen, and I whisper into her ear the words I've spoken to her hundreds of times before but want to make sure she hears one more time: "No matter what, Catherine, if you need me, call. I love you very much."

She whispers back, "I love you, too, Dad."

My daughter turns to go, and I'm speechless as I follow her to her car. As she backs out of our driveway, I watch. She turns her face, smiles that beautiful smile of hers, and with a wave of her hand, she's gone.

It's now evening, and Julie and I take a walk, holding hands. We're quiet and pensive. We've reached another milestone in our lives and, hopefully, we have many miles yet to go.

A Walk on the Beach

ONCE AGAIN, IT'S MY BIRTHDAY, and I find myself walking a familiar path along the ocean in sunny Florida.

Strolling along the beach on the anniversary of my birth has become a sacred ritual over the years—one that only illness or some other act of God or nature can prevent.

While each birthday is important, this year is my 60th, so my walk has a special feel to it. As long as I can remember, I've had a warm feeling about birthdays stemming from the fact that my parents always made a big deal about each and every one of my big days. It's probably no wonder, then, that I attempt to elevate my birthday to a level above all other days. It's not just because I want to celebrate; it's also because I want to remember.

To understand this more fully, you have to know that this long stretch of beach is a place my parents loved dearly. They took me here each year of my childhood on their annual summer vacation. No day in Florida during those two weeks was complete without a walk along the beach with my father. On some occasions, my mother would come along, but mostly it was just my dad and me, and that made our daily walks special and meaningful.

When I was a child, he held my hand, and as I grew older, he let me walk alongside him, unencumbered by his grasp. There were times when we talked to each other as we made our long line of prints in the sand, but what I remember most was the silence. My father, never a verbose man, simply strolled along the water's edge, his only child by his side, his thoughts kept to himself.

This was no awkward silence, though. It was entirely comfortable. In fact, our silence spoke volumes to me. It was as if my father was encouraging me to listen to the sound of the waves as they rolled over our feet, or to take notice of the gulls hovering over our heads. It was like he was urging me to turn inward and listen to the many thoughts that filled my mind.

If that was my father's intention, it worked. Early on, I remember becoming acutely aware of my surroundings; feeling the wind and sun on my bare skin and hearing the crash of the waves and the squawking of the gulls. And later, I started becoming more aware of my thoughts. As I strolled alongside my father, I began to understand what makes us all so unique—our innermost thoughts and feelings.

Occasionally, I would share these newborn bursts of thought with my dad, but mostly I simply let them flow over me, like the waves sweeping over my feet.

Although his death brought an end to the walks I took with my beloved father, as I make my way along the water's edge on this particular day, he is still very much with me. I step across the sand, gazing at the usual sun-worshipers and swimmers, and I realize that the man I loved so much during those walks was as old as I am now!

I recall a strong, erect, and proud man, his warm smile pervading my inner thoughts. "Happy birthday, son!" he tells me, and in response, I reflect on all the good times we shared together.

On this, the 60th anniversary of my birth, I am happy.

～ PART III

End of Life

Over the years, nothing has stirred the emotions in readers more than my columns on death and dying. Perhaps the reason has to do with the fact that although we all die, it is how we die that's different. We are curious, fearful, and intrigued by the process.

Most young physicians have little or no experience with death when they enter the field of medicine. They have to grow up quickly, though, for they suddenly find themselves placed into the maelstrom of life's greatest drama.

It is through these profound experiences that we physicians come to understand our crucial role in the lives of others. Many lessons are learned, many are taught, but most often, we find that the greatest teachers with respect to death and dying are our patients.

At other times, however, we simply learn from those whom we love the most.

A Peaceful Death

IT USED TO BE DIFFERENT. Years ago, major milestones such as birth and death occurred in the home. Women rarely went to hospitals to have their babies, and those who were dying did so in their own beds.

There was a good reason for this: Hospitals had little to offer patients before the modern age of medicine. Today things are different. The facts speak for themselves—70 percent of elderly Americans pass away in hospitals and nursing homes.

I know all too well the drama of the emergency room, the resuscitative efforts, the doctors and nurses shooing out loving family members, and finally, the pronouncement of death. So it was helpful to me last October to witness death as it *should* occur for our elderly loved ones—at home with peace and dignity.

❧ ❧ ❧

The autumn sun was warm and the morning wind crisp on the day my beloved mother died. I knew the end of her life was near as I drove to her home that day. I had watched her slowly deteriorate over the past three years since my father had passed away, and I knew that she had lost her will to live.

I sat on the edge of her bed and kissed her forehead while I held her hand. She looked frail and weak, yet still alert. As if she knew this was to be her last day on earth, she wanted to know what day it was. I told her. And, of course, she unselfishly asked me how *I* was doing. I told her that, too.

I noticed her breathing become more labored, her pulse weakening. "I love you," I said, as moisture filled my eyes.

"I love you, too," she replied. Then she asked me to help her turn to her side, which I did.

I opened the sliding-glass door to let the sun and breeze fill her room, and I switched on her favorite classical music. Then I returned to her bedside.

"I want to go to sleep now," she said, and slowly closed her eyes. I sat there a while longer, looking at this remarkable woman who had brought me into the world; nurtured and loved me; and been my friend, confidant, and support for longer than I could remember.

After so many years, this was to be our last day together.

No doctors rushed to her side as her heart stopped an hour later; no emergency pages were heard overhead; no resuscitation carts were wheeled into her room; no strangers milled about her bed to pronounce her dead.

It was as it should be: My mother died in her familiar bed without pain, being held by the son who worshiped her.

This should happen more often.

Cause of Death: Grief

HAVING BEEN A PHYSICIAN for more than 30 years, I've pronounced many patients dead and have filled out dozens of death certificates detailing the cause of death. But it was different this time. Because my mother died at home, a policeman was sent to the house that afternoon to ascertain that information. It was the law.

"What was the cause of death?" he asked, poised to fill out a form attached to a clipboard.

"A broken heart," I responded.

"Sorry," he replied, "that's not on my list."

I tried again. "Grief was the cause of my mother's death." That would not do either. "Well, what about natural causes?" I asked. Finally, we settled on the generic "cardiac arrest" as the cause of my beloved mother's demise. Satisfied, the officer finished his work and departed.

That diagnosis may have satisfied the legal requirements, but it was certainly not the truth as I knew it. My mother died of a broken heart, of overwhelming grief over the loss of her husband, my father, who had died three years earlier.

Married in Germany on December 25, 1936, they had formed a loving bond that helped sustain them for 52 years. Immigrating to America during the Holocaust, surviving poverty and depression during the early years and occasional bouts of serious illness during the later years, my parents managed to build a home, raise their son, make good friends, and create a full and rich life for themselves.

They were devoted to each other, doing almost everything together. They held hands as they strolled, and kissed while they danced. They were in love, and it was fun to be with them and to share in their joy.

Coming from the "old school," today my father's way of dealing with my mother might be called almost paternal. He was clearly the boss. He handled the money, paid the bills, and planned vacations and evenings out on the town, while my mother stayed at home and took care of her family.

However, my parents were happy with their lives and with their arrangement, and they depended on each other. After my father's retirement, they were almost inseparable. They swam together, ate their meals together, and shopped together.

So I guess I shouldn't have been surprised when, after my father's death at the age of 85, my mother seemed to die as well, never to regain the spark and glow she once possessed. During the first year, she lost most of her eyesight. Nothing seemed to bring her joy, not even visits from her grand-children.

Numerous visits to doctors failed to elicit any definitive diagnosis. Medicines were of no avail. Over the next two years, despite round-the-clock nurses, she slowly lost weight, narrowing her world to her apartment, then to her bedroom chair, and finally to her bed.

At age 83, she finally closed her eyes and died.

I was with her on the sun-filled autumn day that was to be her last. I listened to her heart and lungs with my stetho-scope. They were normal. She did not have an infection, nor was she afflicted with cancer or a stroke. She was not anemic or suffering from kidney disease.

The long and short of it was simple. As I tried to explain to the policeman that afternoon, my mother died . . . of grief.

There should be a place on the certificate for that cause of death.

Just Through Christmas

I HAD BEEN ASSIGNED to The City of Hope, a hospital located in a small city outside of Los Angeles. Patients with advanced stages of cancer were sent there in an attempt to either find some treatment that might cure them, or at least slow down the cancer that was bringing them closer to the brink of death.

It was the day after Christmas, 1969, and I had been on call since the morning of December 23.

I remember being pleasantly surprised to note how few patients had been admitted to our emergency room, and how few telephone calls I had taken from our large community of cancer patients. I was hoping that this slow pace would continue, but it was not to be. From the early-morning hours until late that evening, the sick and dying poured into our hospital. All of our previously empty beds were quickly being taken up, making it increasingly difficult to find rooms for patients during the latter part of the day.

What amazed me most wasn't that our nearly empty hospital filled up so quickly on the day after Christmas, but that the patients appeared more seriously ill than usual and were much closer to death than those patients I'd been admitting over the past six months.

By sunrise the next day, I had pronounced more patients dead than I could ever remember having done during such a short period of time.

Later, I discussed this phenomenon with several of my professors and was told that the increase in admissions of dying patients after a holiday was a common occurrence. It seemed that patients living with a diagnosis of terminal cancer had the will and determination to hold on until a special day. That special day could be a birthday or anniversary, a reunion with a loving relative who lived far away, or a holiday such as Christmas.

Having been in the medical profession for nearly 30 years, I have to say that this will to live doesn't surprise me. Although I've seen it many times since that Christmas in California many years ago, I've often wondered what it is about the human spirit that makes this phenomenon possible.

The answer is now clear to me. Just knowing that staying alive a little longer will allow us to love and be loved one more time seems to be a key factor in staying alive. Love has never been given enough credit by the health-care profession, yet it may be the ingredient that does more for restoring health than many potent medicines.

The smile of a child when he sees his parents at his bedside, resulting in the stabilization of his pulse and blood pressure readings, or a patient coming out of a seemingly hopeless and prolonged coma after weeks of round-the-clock care by loved ones, are just two of the many examples of how love can affect our health.

Recent scientific studies have even shown that when there's someone at home to give comfort, love, and support to a person who's recently suffered a heart attack, that individual has a significantly lower chance of having a second attack than those who go home to an empty house.

In many ways, it is love that gives all of us the strength—as well as the will—to carry on.

Myths of Miscarriage

WHILE THERE HAS BEEN MUCH DEBATE and discussion on the subject of abortion (the elective interruption of an *unwanted* pregnancy), very little is heard about miscarriage (the spontaneous loss of a *wanted* pregnancy).

As an obstetrician who deals with patients who miscarry on an all-too-frequent basis, and as a husband and father who has lost a child through miscarriage, I wish to correct this imbalance.

While approximately 15 percent of all known early pregnancies result in miscarriage, it's estimated that if the studies include those women who get pregnant but miscarry before the pregnancy can be confirmed, approximately half of all pregnant women miscarry. Regardless of the percentage used, the fact remains that many couples endure this type of loss.

There are those who believe that the early cessation of pregnancy through miscarriage is less traumatic than the loss of a child already born. My experience does not confirm that impression. The loss of even a small number of cells growing inside the uterus can be cause for considerable anguish.

Incredibly, a woman does not have to actually miscarry to feel this sense of loss.

For example, a woman expecting twins was referred to me when she was approximately 20 weeks along. She was very excited about the prospect of bringing two lives into her family. However, after repeating the ultrasound exam (which had originally been performed at another hospital), we noted that an error had been made. What appeared to be two fetuses on the earlier exam was in fact only one.

Carefully, I explained that she had never had twins inside her body, but that the one child she *did* carry appeared healthy and was growing normally. However, after perceiving herself to be expecting twins, the knowledge that there was only one child created a loss in her mind that caused considerable depression and turmoil.

❖ ❖ ❖

In addition to the pain that parents feel after enduring such a loss, there is also the issue of insensitivity, which many have to deal with when notifying family and friends. Ask any woman who has miscarried about the comments that these well-meaning people make after she's lost a baby, and she'll tell you that she hears things such as: "You can always get pregnant again," "It was for the best," or "It isn't like it was a real child yet."

Unfortunately, none of these statements are necessarily true, nor do they ease the woman's pain. And make no mistake about it, there *is* pain—and if it is not dealt with immediately, it can last for years, often surfacing later on as depression, guilt, and insecurity.

We grieve for much in our lives, especially the loss of our loved ones. As a rule, society recognizes that type of loss, offering support in many ways. However, society should not forget that "loved ones" also includes those lost through miscarriage.

Life After Death

IT WAS 1969, a time when our country was experiencing great turmoil, excitement, and change. We were in the midst of the Vietnam War, which was traumatic indeed, but we had also just landed two men on the moon, inspiring pride and hope.

It was also a time of new beginnings in my own life.

I was to begin my studies at The City of Hope hospital in California. I had finished my formal training in OB/GYN and wanted to focus on the aspect of gynecology that dealt with malignant tumors.

This huge medical complex was appropriately named, for hope could be felt everywhere you went. For example, the chief of staff/professor of surgery made rounds with young doctors and nurses each day, often quoting relevant Bible verses as easily as he did medical facts. He brought feeling of faith and confidence with him as he looked in on each patient.

Outside each hospital room window, the most colorful and beautiful flowers could be seen, and hummingbird feeders attracted hungry little birds that were a delight to watch. On the hospital grounds, there was also a house of prayer.

But what was most memorable about The City of Hope was that we (the other young doctors and I) were encouraged to really be attentive to our patients—talking with them about their lives, their desires, and their fears. Our Bible-quoting professor told us that by doing so, both student and patient would gain much. How right he was.

I met Elizabeth on my first day at work. She was 25 years old and had cervical cancer. Despite primary treatment involving a radical hysterectomy and subsequent radiation, the tumor had continued to spread. Elizabeth had been sent to The City of Hope as a last resort, a common theme among our hundreds of patients with cancer.

During my rounds, I often found myself sitting by her bedside, just listening. She talked of many things during those last three months of her life, but mostly she opened up about her fear of death. What she brought up the most was her fear that there was nothing after death, and that her life, by ending so early, left no legacy, no memories—nothing of lasting value.

I told her how, in medical school, after dissecting my first cadaver, I had peered at every muscle, organ, artery, vein and nerve, and came to realize that whatever existed after death did not involve our Earthly body. I explained that I did not believe in a vindictive or punitive God, and therefore it was difficult for me to believe in a heaven or hell. But I did believe in "life after death" through the continuation of life itself.

I shared my belief that the essence of our being lived on long after we died, that the good or bad in our lives affected those around us, and thus lived on in them. The role modeling, principles, character, and morality we displayed would be transmitted to our children, our relatives, and our friends in an everlasting fashion.

My explanation seemed to bring her some solace. Elizabeth started to believe that despite her young age and the fact that she was childless, she had indeed touched many lives in a very positive manner and that the effect of these interactions would live on long after she passed away. She found comfort in this type of life after death.

Medically, we did not have much else to offer Elizabeth, so I was glad I could offer her some comfort during our talks. The concept of life after death that we discussed so long ago at The City of Hope did something else: It brought *me* comfort as well.

A *Last Word*

IN ORDER TO MINIMIZE many serious end-of-life issues, Americans have been encouraged to make a living will. After attending a funeral recently, I came to the conclusion that not only should we *sign* a living will, but we should also leave behind a *last word*. In case you've never heard of a last word, I will explain by relating a story.

Sylvia Haffkine was 93 years old when she died. She was an exceptional woman who lived life to its fullest. When she passed away, she left my dear friend Ron, her only child, heartbroken. Sylvia and Ron had always had a close, loving, and nurturing relationship.

While planning his mother's funeral, Ron expressed a desire to deliver her eulogy because he felt that he not only knew his mother better than anyone else, but also believed this would be an important part of his own healing process.

As the time grew near for Ron to deliver his speech, he grew concerned and anxious. What could he say about his mother to adequately paint a picture of her life and their love for each other? And, even if he did find the right words, would he be able to maintain his composure to be able to verbalize them?

As Ron lovingly sifted through his mother's possessions, he found his answer. His mother had left him a letter written several years earlier that she had sealed in an envelope. The outside read: "To be opened upon my passing." Sylvia had left Ron her *last word*.

After reading his mother's letter, Ron's anxiety over what he would say, and if he could say it, disappeared. In addition, much of his grief dissipated. Sylvia's last word brought her only child comfort and peace.

The next morning, on a sunny, beautifully crisp autumn day, several dozen friends and family members gathered at

Sylvia's grave site. Slowly, but with determination, Ron rose to speak. I was nervous. I knew nothing of Sylvia's letter, only of Ron's earlier concerns. I was hoping that my friend, a sensitive and emotional man, would find the proper words to lay his mother to rest. I need not have worried.

Ron stood straight and tall, and with a warm smile on his face told us about Sylvia's letter. He said that nothing he could say could better explain who his mother was or what she had meant to him. Then he read the letter.

Sylvia told her son not to mourn her loss, but to remember her life. She said her death was a loss, but surely not a tragedy. She had lived long and well, made better and richer because of Ron. She instructed her son to continue to lead a life filled with laughter, goodness, and fun; to always find satisfaction in the present; and to feel positive anticipation for the future.

Most important, she told her only child how proud she was of him, how happy he had made her, and that she loved him with all her heart and soul.

❖ ❖ ❖

We leave behind a living will to inform our loved ones about our final wishes just in case we're unable to speak for ourselves during a serious illness. Legal wills also let them know how we wish to distribute all we've accumulated during our lives. It would follow, then, that we would also want to leave a last word.

Last words provide closure—they signify the end of a physical life and a beginning of a spiritual one. Last words can also help soothe old grievances by extending or asking for forgiveness. And they can be words of praise, love, guidance, and support.

I think that we would all be served well to put our last words down on paper and to place this document in a safe place so it can be found at the appropriate time.

What a beautiful and considerate gift to leave our loved ones.

Taking Her Turn

SEVERAL YEARS AGO while discussing a dear friend who had recently been diagnosed with metastatic cancer, I somberly mentioned to my mother-in-law, Dorothy, that it was now our friend's turn. Asked what I meant by that, I explained that someday each of us would be faced with impending death, and when that day came, it would be our "turn."

We talked about how our turn sometimes comes very quickly—for example, in the wake of a massive heart attack—but that at other times the end could be quite drawn out, as in the case of a chronic illness.

I told Dorothy that at some point in our lives—as sure as the sun rises and sets each day—we will find ourselves at home plate, be given a bat, and be told that it's our turn. How we handle that situation has always intrigued me.

Therefore, it was particularly meaningful to me on a winter day in 1995 when Dorothy—having just had a chest x-ray revealing the ominous finding of cancer—turned to me with tears in her eyes and said, "It's my turn."

Now, as you're probably aware, how people handle impending death has been the subject of numerous works. As far as I'm concerned, the most probing is Elisabeth Kübler-Ross's book *On Death and Dying*. In considerable detail, the author delineates the various stages that most individuals go through. These phases often include denial, shock, disbelief, anger, bargaining with God, depression, and finally, acceptance.

From the beginning, it seemed that Dorothy was an exception to Kübler-Ross's stages, having moved quickly and directly from diagnosis to acceptance. Perhaps it was because she was no stranger to grief, having endured the premature deaths of her mother, brother, sister, and nephew, as well as the death of her beloved husband of 38 years, Eddie.

Never complaining despite great discomfort, Dorothy only seemed interested in how those around her were coping.

"You need to sleep (or eat, or rest, or take better care of yourself)," were just a few of her loving admonitions to her friends and family members. She did not want to be a burden to anyone.

One evening at dinner, when she was obviously in great pain, Dorothy related to me how proud she was of her achievements in life. Having had a loving marriage; four devoted children and eight beautiful grandchildren; and hundreds of relatives, dear friends, and admirers, she said she was filled with pride and love.

In addition, she listed the countless charities and organizations she had worked for, good deeds she had accomplished, and causes she had supported with her time and resources. Tearfully and with regret, she also acknowledged, "But there is so much more I want to do."

Dorothy had always told me how, above all, she wanted to make a difference in the world, and I was pleased that she was able to acknowledge that her life had indeed made an impact on others.

Watching Dorothy gracefully "take her turn" made me realize how I want to take mine. She hit a grand-slam home run, right out of the park and into our hearts and souls.

Dorothy's Final Days

WHILE READING AN ARTICLE on death and dying in the *New York Times Magazine*, I found a quote by Ira Byock of Missoula, Montana, which not only intrigued me, but also brought back the powerful memory of my mother-in-law Dorothy's death.

Byock, an active hospice worker, wrote, "For the dying, the last days can bring with them a heightened awareness, contentment, connectedness. The transition from life to death can be as beautiful and profound as the miracle of birth."

Dorothy's last 48 hours exemplified the truth in Byock's words, especially the part about heightened awareness. Riddled with cancer, Dorothy's body and mind were slowly drifting away, despite fervent attempts by her doctors to halt the disease's progress. For months, she had lain on her couch enduring the latest chemotherapy treatment, as well as drugs used to curb her pain. Slowly, her usually effervescent and bubbly personality faded away.

Attempting to stimulate her into conversation became increasingly difficult as she lay on the couch, slipping into a barely lucid state. We were unable to do anything more than hold her hand, kiss her forehead, and whisper loving words into her ear.

I missed the long talks we used to have—missed listening to her uniquely spirited perceptions about life, and her penchant for telling it like it was. Sleeping most of the day became the norm, and we all resigned ourselves to the fact that Dorothy's energy, as well as her clarity of speech, thought, and purpose were now gone.

We were wrong.

Spending all day, every day, at her mother's home, my wife, Julie, was already up and dressed when the call came at 6:45 A.M. "Come now!" was the terse message that Dorothy uttered to her daughter.

Julie accelerated her usual morning ritual and arrived at her mother's bedside minutes later. Sitting up in bed that morning, Dorothy steadily and pointedly instructed Julie to bring her loved ones to her side. She seemed alert, determined, and oriented.

Julie had not seen her mother this way in months. Dorothy had obviously decided to embark on her final journey, and she wanted to say good-bye to her loved ones. A son in New York, a daughter and son-in-law in Kentucky, and a son and daughter-in-law in Nashville were all called and told to "come now."

I received the message while on rounds at the hospital. Dropping everything, I hurried to my car and to the awaiting drama occurring just a few miles away.

Little by little, Dorothy's friends and relatives arrived. They knelt at her bedside, trying to find the right words for this special moment. They were aware that Dorothy was listening to them intently, absorbing their words. A box filled with tissues slowly emptied as the day progressed. By mid-afternoon, the stream of visitors ended, and Dorothy was once again surrounded only by her children and a few close friends.

Dorothy appeared satisfied that she had accomplished what she had set out to do. She had somehow summoned the energy to gather her loved ones around her so she could give them each a last word or hug.

By that evening, as each of us held a part of Dorothy's frail and weakened body, she slowly began to slip back into the world from which she had roused herself, never opening her eyes again, never speaking another word.

Dorothy passed away 36 hours later.

❖ ❖ ❖

I have told this story of Dorothy's last moment of clarity and awareness to many since her death. I was truly amazed and touched by what I had witnessed. How could someone so close to death, so weak and frail, so filled with pain and disease, suddenly sit up in bed and announce her wishes with such purpose and forthrightness?

Perhaps like the second wind experienced by a long-distance runner, or the inexplicable demonstration of super-human strength displayed by someone at a moment of crisis, all of Dorothy's brain cells, though drugged, sedated, and dying, were able to unite in one last burst of energy to awaken her senses and allow her to say her final farewell.

Although I've been a part of the medical profession for more than 35 years, I'm still amazed by the human spirit and its sense of purpose. My colleagues and I also marvel at the intuitiveness of our patients when they think they're going to die. We really pay attention to those last words, because we know that our patients are often aware of something that we're not.

Dorothy knew that death was near on that fateful morning, and she empowered herself to grasp one last moment of awareness and purpose.

On March 29, 1996, Dorothy Goldstein died in the same way that she had lived—surrounded by those who loved her.

Coping with Grief

THE WELL-WISHERS, FRIENDS, AND FAMILY were gone now, and the house was quiet. It was a respite that this man sorely needed. His beloved wife of 52 years had died just five days earlier, and since then it had been nonstop funeral plans, well-meaning visitors, and sleepless nights.

He was alone now, walking through the home he and his wife had shared. Each photograph, piece of furniture, and item of clothing was a reminder of the woman he had loved as much as life itself. He lay down on his bed fully clothed, not even taking off his shoes, and closed his eyes, unable to imagine how life could go on without his precious mate.

His children found him lying on the bed the next morning, his eyes still closed. He's in a peaceful slumber, they thought at first, but then they quickly realized that their father had died. An autopsy later revealed a massive heart attack.

❖ ❖ ❖

How often have we heard these words: "I can't live without her (or him)". . . "If something happened to you, I don't think I could go on living—the pain would be too great". . . or "Life without you would be unbearable."

Do we really believe this when we hear it or say it? Well, a study I read recently shed some light on this question. It reported that at times, grief can be so overwhelming and stressful that it *can* lead to serious illness or death.

At a cardiovascular epidemiology conference sponsored by the American Medical Association, Dr. Murray A. Mittleman of Deaconess Hospital in Boston presented the findings of interviews with 1,774 heart attack patients shortly after they were afflicted.

These patients were asked whether any close relatives or friends had died during the preceding six months. The researchers found that nine of the patients had experienced the death of someone they loved one day before the heart attack, a rate 14 times more than is expected. Nine other patients sustained heart attacks on the second and third days after the death of a loved one.

The study concluded that approximately one percent (18 of 1,774) of the heart attacks were probably triggered by the death of a loved one. If there is a direct cause and effect, it would mean that of the 1.5 million Americans who have heart attacks each year, 15,000 are the direct result of the death of a loved one immediately preceding the attack.

Stress is considered a risk factor leading to diminished heart function, so it is not so difficult to believe that losing someone you love deeply—a spouse of many years or a child—could result in heart attack or death.

Physicians have seen grieving patients lose their desire to eat, their ability to sleep, and their will to go on living. We have witnessed the tears, depression, and pain of those who survive, and frequently wonder if there is anything we can do to help. The reality, however, is that there is little anyone can do for those who have lost a loved one other than to say, "I am so sorry," and to show compassion, friendship, and support.

The elderly seem especially vulnerable to such life-altering events. Sharing a life with a spouse for decades often results in such a closeness that it is often difficult to envision one without the other. Couples are not just joined at the hip, as the old saying goes, but frequently are joined at the heart as well. Just as the complicated surgical process of separating conjoined twins often results in the passing of one or both, so too does it occur when long-united couples are separated by death.

When we love someone for years and years, that person becomes part of our being, soul, and heart. It is no wonder, then, that when that love is taken away, our being, soul, and heart are vulnerable to dying as well.

In order to help those who are left alone after a loved one's passing, we really need to pay more attention to the debilitating effects of grief.

When Good-bye Really Means Good-bye

MANY RHETORICAL PHRASES are part of our daily lives. From "How are you doing?" and "What's going on?" to "See you," we often utter these statements without really wanting or expecting an in-depth answer.

"Fine, how are you?" "Nothing much," and "Okay, see you later" are perfectly appropriate responses. However, sometimes these words and phrases can have a special meaning and significance.

I first realized this one summer while attending a camp reunion. In a very perfunctory way, I casually asked an old acquaintance whom I had not seen in many years how she was doing. I was not expecting the answer I received.

Suffering from metastatic breast cancer, this woman openly and quite willingly explained in detail *exactly* how she was doing (or more precisely how she was *not* doing). Fifteen somewhat difficult minutes later, I realized that my question had been anything but casual to her.

Similarly, seemingly routine statements and questions can end up being significant for the parties on both ends. Such was the case recently when I telephoned a friend suffering from cancer.

I had known Eleanor for many years and had spent considerable time with her and her husband. I had grown very fond of this intelligent, energetic, successful, and remarkable individual, so I wanted to call and say that I was thinking about her at this most stressful and difficult time.

What I got from the call, however, was as meaningful for me as I hope it was for Eleanor. Her husband, Randy, picked up the phone when I called, and we chatted for a while. Suddenly and unexpectedly, he said, "Let me put Eleanor on the speakerphone so that you can talk to her directly."

Having heard that Eleanor was close to death and not responding to many of those around her, I was pleasantly surprised when I heard that friendly, strong voice of hers say, "Hi, Frank." Our brief conversation ended with a phrase that was not meaningless in any sense to either one of us.

"Good-bye, Frank," she said warmly.

"Good-bye, Eleanor," I responded in an equally heartfelt fashion.

Tears filled my eyes as I placed the phone in its cradle, knowing that this time, *good-bye* truly meant "good-bye." There would be no more greetings or sign-offs for Eleanor and me. Six days later, she died quietly and painlessly in her sleep surrounded by her loving husband and children.

I learned that the term *good-bye* originally stemmed from 16th-century English and means "God be with you." How fitting and proper that Eleanor and I both realized how much meaning our simple good-byes really had.

May God be with you, Eleanor. I'll always remember you.

The Right to Live

YOU HEAR MUCH IN TODAY'S MEDIA about an individual's right to die. Unfortunately, there is little spoken or written about the other side of that coin . . . the right to live.

Medical journals and the lay press fill up pages of text on physician-assisted suicide, euthanasia, death with dignity, living wills, durable power of attorney, and organ donation. We have been schooled in how to kill ourselves through the book *Final Exit,* how to let others help decide under what conditions we are to die by signing advanced directives, how to sign up for organ donations at the time of our demise, and what our attitude toward living beyond our productive and fulfilling years should be.

And yet, there are those who are skeptical about these issues. Some are fearful that the medical profession will be just a little too eager to avoid resuscitation because of disease or age, a little too quick to turn off the respirators to reduce costs or to procure much needed organs for other patients. Many are fearful that if physician-assisted suicide is legalized, it would lead to a slippery slope to unrequested euthanasia.

There is evidence that these concerns are real. Studies in the Netherlands, where physician-assisted suicide is legal, have found that physicians taking care of the elderly and seriously disabled in nursing homes prefer euthanasia in cases where physical limitations prohibits a patient from taking his or her own life. Many fear that physicians will be able to yield too much power over choice in this arena of life and death.

But what about the right to live? With an ever-increasing elderly population, there are many who are truly concerned that despite an intense desire to continue with the life they're living, there will be subtle and not-so-subtle pressures imposed on them by society as a whole and the medical profession as a group to dishonor these wishes.

I was made acutely aware of this dilemma recently when a close friend's 102-year-old mother, who required stitches to close a head wound inflicted by a fall at home, was taken to a nearby emergency room. During the minor operation, my friend's mother, who still had her faculties and continued to find joy in her daily activities, suddenly suffered cardiorespiratory arrest. What followed was not the usual quick response by the treating surgeon to begin cardiopulmonary resuscitation, but rather a hesitancy to do anything to correct the problem.

Perhaps this was due to the woman's age and the fact that the physician did not know his new patient and made assumptions that were not accurate. Whatever the reason for the hesitancy, the much-needed lifesaving techniques were not immediately initiated. Fortunately, a close friend (and a practicing physician) who was with my friend at the hospital, saw what was happening and quickly began the chest-compression techniques that, within a relatively short period of time, brought this elderly woman back to life.

Later, when I was informed of what had occurred earlier that day, I was reminded that when there are decisions to be made as to whether medical treatment should occur, the quality of one's life and the desire to continue with that life should be measured by the patient and their loved ones—not solely by the physician.

A few weeks following this emergency-room event, my friend's mother fell once more, this time breaking her hip. Again, she found herself in the hospital, but her hip was successfully repaired, and she is now recuperating comfortably, with her beloved son by her side.

Yes, this woman is very old and frail, and her remaining days are few, but she is loved dearly and brings her son much joy, as he does her. She wants to live, and she has that right.

❧ ❧ ❧

An Angel Named Alexander

THE LITTLE BOY DID WHAT HE ALWAYS DID on weekday mornings. He finished his breakfast, put on his jacket, said good-bye to his mom, and headed out the door to the waiting car pool that would take him to school.

But on this January morning, ten-year-old Alexander Martin also did something that was a bit uncustomary. When he was halfway out the door, he turned around and ran back to his mother, who was standing in the kitchen.

"I need a kiss," he told her.

His mother smiled as she knelt down to hug and kiss her youngest son.

"I love you," he said as he turned to leave once again.

"I love you, too," she responded.

Little did Alexander's mother know on that cold winter morning that the loving words she bestowed upon her son would be the last she would ever utter to him. And little did Alexander know that he had just given his mother an incredible gift that would be forever treasured and remembered.

Later that day, Alexander collapsed while at school and slipped into a coma. Seven days later, he died.

❖ ❖ ❖

Born with a congenital heart defect, Alexander was anything but frail. He participated in every possible sport and was constantly on the move. Even in class, he couldn't sit still. Asked by his teacher once to stop fidgeting, he responded with his usual endearing charm: "I can't help it. I've got to move." Although heart failure may have stopped Alexander Martin from moving, nothing will ever stop the flow of memories his family and friends share about this extraordinary little boy.

From the day he was born, it was clear to all who came into contact with Alexander that there was something different about him. This special little boy who adored his brothers and worshiped his parents was a true gift from God. His parents regarded him as an angel sent by Heaven to be with their family. His oft-visited pediatrician called him "Alexander the Great," and his teachers credited him with showing them how to be better at their job.

Alexander could strike up a conversation with anyone—no matter how young or old—at any time. Friends of the family, some of whom admitted that they didn't particularly care for children, were nonetheless attracted to this child.

Even as he lay unconscious in his hospital bed at Vanderbilt Children's Hospital, unable to speak, his angelic demeanor seemed to reach out to the many nurses and doctors who treated him, and they immediately felt a unique connection develop.

As if he had lived 80 years or more, Alexander's funeral attracted thousands of people who felt the need to embrace the family. "It took God seven days to create heaven and earth, and all that is within, and it also took seven days for God to take my son back to him," his dad told me one night. "He will always be that perfect child for all of us who knew and loved him."

Alexander's ten short years on earth exemplify the saying that it is not the *length* of one's days that matters, it is the *quality* of those days that truly count. Alexander's short life certainly counted. To him, life was a team sport. Never one to like sitting on the bench, Alexander was, and probably still is, very much in the game.

Because of Alexander, I make it a point to end each phone conversation or interaction with my wife and children with those same words that Alexander spoke to his mother as he hurried off to school that day: "I love you."

Perhaps Alexander's gift to his mother should be a wake-up call and reminder for all of us to do the same.

~ PART IV

A Personal Point of View

We physicians are an opinionated group. Although we may have medicine in common, oftentimes, that may be all we have in common.

Over the years, I've had the opportunity to express my personal point of view on a wide variety of issues. From columns on subjects as diverse as abortion, parenting issues, women's concerns, forgiveness, depression, and friendship, I've told it like I see it—which you'll see for yourself in the essays that follow.

The Unending Controversy

SHE WAS ONLY 21 YEARS OLD, yet she was dying. However, in spite of the many tubes entering her body, the lack of makeup, and the critical condition she was in, I could see her beauty.

Her despondent parents sitting nearby showed me photographs of her prior to her illness, and I could see that she was a lovely young woman. But there was more. I could also see the hope and purpose in her face. I felt certain that she'd had big dreams for her future that included a career, marriage, a nice home, children, and grandchildren.

Unfortunately, since I also knew that she would soon die, a hopelessness crept through my body. There was nothing that all the advances in medicine could do to change the fact that this senseless death was going to occur.

It was 1968, five years before Roe v. Wade made abortion a private matter between a woman, her doctor, and her conscience. My young and beautiful patient had conceived out of wedlock and had obtained what she thought was her only alternative—an illegal abortion.

Tragically, that process had been improperly and criminally performed. On the night she arrived in our emergency room with a temperature of 105 degrees and in septic shock, an x-ray revealed a wire rod imbedded not just in her abdominal cavity, but also in her right lung. It had been inserted through the uterus two days prior in an attempt to induce abortion.

Despite a hysterectomy and the strongest antibiotics available, she remained in a coma, from which she would never recover. A brilliant student and a vivacious, popular coed, she had gotten pregnant, felt she could not tell her parents, and had sought out the advice of friends.

Each day at our hospital (prior to the landmark court decision of 1973), we admitted women who had been victimized by improperly performed abortions and who needed urgent care to recover. The lucky patients did well after treatment. This patient was not so lucky.

I was only 28 years old at the time, and to me, this young woman was more than just a patient—she was a peer. She was like a friend I had known somewhere else, in some other time. My shift was over, yet I sat at her bedside holding her limp, cool hand, unable to leave.

Her parents, with tears staining their faces, stared in speechless disbelief at their beloved daughter. It was all like a movie—none of it seemed quite real. When their daughter's heart stopped, we tried to revive her, but the muscle and valves of her heart were also infected, and our vigorous attempts failed.

As I pulled the sheet over her face and pronounced her dead, I knew that our system of dealing with a pregnant woman who couldn't continue her pregnancy needed to undergo change.

❧ ❧ ❧

Today, as it was then, abortion remains an extremely sensitive topic because it is a no-win situation. There seems to be no middle ground. It is an issue deeply rooted in an individual's concept of life. There are those who oppose abortion because they believe it to be murder, and there are those who are pro-choice because they believe that life begins at birth.

The entire issue pivots on the question of when one believes life begins, but since no legal or medical authority will ever have the definitive answer, we are left with an unending controversy.

There are actually three sides to the abortion issue, not two. There are the two adamant and vocal extremist groups: one protesting abortion at clinics, burning and harassing abortion centers, and shooting doctors in the back; the other a group also protesting at clinics, claiming that women should have no limitations on what they do with their body or fetus.

The extremists are unrelenting and uncompromising, and each group makes up approximately 15 percent of the American public. It is also these two sides that we read about in our newspapers and see on our TV sets.

The third side is represented by the approximately 70 percent of Americans who do not relish the concept or act of abortion, but who also believe that since it is always going to be a reality, society should allow women to choose for themselves.

Many in this last group, however, also believe that certain limitations on abortion are appropriate. Parental notification, 24-hour waiting periods, and gestational age limits are a few examples.

One thing is very clear: Roe v. Wade did more to reduce pregnancy-related mortality than any other medical advance since blood transfusion and antibiotics surfaced in obstetrics. It's difficult for me to think about going back to those days when women risked their lives to end a situation that they couldn't deal with.

Sure, She's Depressed

RESEARCH CONDUCTED by the American Psychological Association has found that women are twice as likely to suffer from depression than men. I'm not surprised.

As an obstetrician, I've been able to study certain female characteristics and behavior from a vantage point not shared by men in other professions. My observations have led me to conclude that our society expects too much from modern women, which is why they suffer from depression more than men do. Above anything else, I believe that the overriding problem is that modern women are overwhelmed by overlapping responsibilities related to careers, children, finances, and their mates.

Take the pregnant working wife, for example. Because the majority of my patients fit into this category, I am witness to their daily stresses and strains. Basically, my patients are exhausted.

While all women tire during pregnancy, there is an emotional, as well as a physical, exhaustion that also occurs. Physiologically, the metabolic rate during pregnancy significantly increases, and with the workload on the heart being increased by 50 percent, women find it increasingly more difficult to handle daily routines. Add on the burden of carrying around an extra 35 pounds or so while attempting to fulfill work obligations, and it should come as no surprise that life gets very tiring for the average pregnant woman.

When I've urged my patients to get more rest, they've told me that they're "fine"—they "just sit at a desk all day" or engage in some other type of nonphysical work.

But when you combine duties such as fixing breakfast for the family, dropping loved ones off at school and work, fighting traffic, parking the car, walking to the building, getting to the desk, rushing through lunch, heading home on a congested freeway, shopping in a crowded grocery store, and then preparing dinner for the family . . . even a desk job becomes an arduous task for a woman who has been urged to rest and reduce stress. It's no wonder that women dealing with these stressful situations develop complications of pregnancy such as premature birth, which could have possibly been prevented by reducing their work load.

We need to change our attitude toward women who are pregnant. Our society needs to modify rules and regulations so that women have more opportunity to rest or stop working during pregnancy. We need to be more understanding and compassionate toward those in our society who bear the responsibility of carrying our future citizens in their bodies.

If we do so, then who knows—maybe pregnant women will no longer be so vulnerable to depression.

The Value of Friendship

Approximately 55 years ago, I met five boys in my Nashville kindergarten class. What makes this somewhat unusual is that the other night, I met them for dinner. Somehow, through all these years, our friendship has survived, and we are still in contact with each other.

"The boys," as we call ourselves, began meeting for monthly dinners a few years ago to ensure that we did not let friendships that had spanned more than four decades lapse out of apathy.

I think a lot about friendship these days. As a physician, I am privy to one of the real joys in life each time I see a patient being comforted by a friend. A companion who will hold a patient's hand, listen with sympathy, or just help pass the time with idle conversation can often be as beneficial to someone's recovery as a potent medication.

Friendships are often strengthened in medical facilities. They are watered and fed in our corridors and hospital rooms, and in our cafeterias and chapels. We find friends in many ways, but we often solidify our friendships in times of adversity. During an illness, we often see genuine caring and concern being displayed by others. Being together during times of adversity can permanently bond humans together.

Of course, not everyone can maintain childhood friends, as I've been able to do. People are mobile—they move from city to city or merely change neighborhoods. Yet, regardless of the length of the relationship, we all have a need to make and maintain close friends in our lives.

Lifelong friends come to accept each other as they truly are. Having remained friends for 50-plus years, the "boys" and I take pride in the fact that when we sit around the table, laughing and sharing stories, we're like family. We don't talk much about politics or serious matters, and we rarely talk about our wives, kids, or jobs. We tell jokes, talk about sports, and, of course, reflect on "the good old days." We acknowledge that we're getting older, and we even discuss the inevitability of our deaths.

But whatever the topic, our meetings continue to bring us closer together. We don't meet unless all six of us can be there. Perhaps that speaks about our subconscious, instinctual need to be a circle unbroken, a bond intact.

While there are many uncertainties in life, I do know one thing: When I'm old and sick and lying in my hospital bed bemoaning my predicament, there will be at least five other chairs at my bedside.

That "Good-Look" Feeling

I HAVE A QUESTION: Why are we so hard on ourselves?

I'm not talking about extreme (and illogical) cases of self-deprecation—an example being John Quincy Adams, who at age 70, after serving as Secretary of State, President of the United States, and a member of Congress, wrote, "My whole life has been a succession of disappointments. I can scarcely recollect a single instance of success in anything that I ever undertook." Rather, I'm talking about ordinary people like you and me who don't always feel like we're good enough.

For example, why, after dressing for the day or evening will I sometimes gaze into the mirror of my bathroom and feel that I look good, yet other times, I visualize nothing in my image that looks remotely attractive. Often, I can feel both ways at the same time by just flicking my head one way or another—or just changing mirrors.

The argument I have heard most often with respect to this subject is that if we don't think we look good, it means that we really don't like ourselves. But I just don't buy that theory. Being raised as an only child in a warm, nurturing home where I was loved and respected, I couldn't help but grow up liking myself. I still do. So it can't be that simple.

As a young man, I remember that when I was getting ready to go out on a date, it was crucial to find that "good look" in the mirror just before leaving home. If I didn't get just the right look, I would feel somewhat out of sorts during the entire evening. Many might believe that these aspirations for a certain level of attractiveness apply more to women than men, but I don't agree. (Of course, don't expect a poll of men to reveal any reliable statistics.)

At those times when I don't feel that I look that good, it doesn't seem as if anyone else around me senses this at all—in fact, I may even be complimented on my appearance. My beautiful wife can walk into a room and elicit admiring stares from both sexes, yet she often turns to me and states that she just doesn't feel as if she looks good. If you've ever had the experience of seeing a photo of yourself that inwardly made you cringe in horror—only to have someone say, "What a great picture!" then you know exactly what I'm talking about.

I guess that accepting and living with insecure feelings about oneself is only abnormal or harmful when it falls outside the norm. Surely, the anorexic young woman who, in a quest for that good-look feeling, feels that she can never lose enough weight, represents an extreme case of the self-image issue.

I suppose our vanity is not only normal, but perhaps even healthy. While I don't understand this matter entirely, I do know one thing: No matter how old, wise, successful, or secure I get—I'll always want to look good!

Physician, Heal Thyself

I'VE OFTEN HEARD THAT DOCTORS make the worst patients and are the most difficult to care for.

Having severed my Achilles tendon playing racquetball, which resulted in surgery, a cast on my right leg, and six weeks of crutches followed by a long period of rehabilitation, I now believe this to be true. I was not a "happy camper," and I'm sure that I made life difficult for my family, friends, and colleagues.

From the moment I fell to the court floor that Sunday morning, feeling excruciating pain above my right heel, I knew what had happened and had an idea what was in store for me. I was sure that I'd have to make many significant changes and adjustments in my hectic life.

How right I was. What I did *not* know, however, was how much I would learn from this very unpleasant experience.

Over the past few years, I had increased my level of exercise significantly, pushing myself harder while jogging and weight lifting on a near-daily basis. I was a typical middle-aged body with a 25-year-old mentality. But in an my attempt to deny the aging process, I stopped *listening* to my body, which finally had its say on the racquetball court.

It was a painful way to learn that valuable lesson: Moderation is the key to survival. Had I not suffered this injury, I believe that a more serious consequence would have resulted. I also learned the importance of living in a society that addresses the needs of the physically challenged.

Among other things, being on crutches resulted in a change in my perception of distance. What was once a short walk from my car to my office, was suddenly a painstakingly long span to cover. It was as if I were viewing the world through the wrong side of a pair of binoculars.

Having handicapped parking, ramps, extra-width doors, and adequate rest room facilities at my disposal made my daily passages possible and bearable. I developed a better understanding of what it must have been like before these aids for the handicapped were instituted in our society.

Finally, I learned a lot about how illness or injury can change not only how I perceived myself, but how others perceived me.

Being a very active person, my sudden sedentary life caused me to become easily frustrated and occasionally depressed. I felt vulnerable and considered myself damaged goods. While those around me were very supportive and kind, from my new sitting position I watched and listened as people bent down close to me and with too-loud voices asked how I was doing.

I am not deaf, I thought to myself. I am still not sure why people raise their voices when talking to someone in a cast or wheelchair. Perhaps we subconsciously treat those who are ill or injured in a distant manner—literally.

As I sat in my chair, leg propped up, watching the world revolve around me, I became a more empathetic human being. I believe this experience made me a better person and, hopefully, a better physician. Perhaps the next time life hands me a sudden jolt, I will be more equipped to handle it.

Forgiveness Is Good Medicine

ON AUGUST 28, 1938, Ilse and Ludwig Boehm were two of many immigrants who fled to America to seek a life of freedom. Among the few lucky ones escaping the Holocaust of Nazi Germany, my parents moved to Nashville, Tennessee, where a job and a new life were waiting for them.

They left behind their home, business, family, friends, and memories. They also left behind close relatives and lifelong friends who were tragically put to death in the concentration camps of Europe along with six million other Jews. Therefore, it's not surprising that forgiveness was often a topic of conversation among my parents and their friends when they discussed the almost inconceivable events that occurred at that time.

Those discussions elicited varying opinions with respect to the issue of forgiveness. I heard some espouse the notion that Germany could never be forgiven for what it did to Jews and non-Jews alike. But most of all, I remember my father's viewpoint, which was quite different. His response was always the same: "We can never forget, but we *must* find a way to forgive."

He acknowledged that it would be almost impossible to forgive those Germans who were responsible for the unbelievable crimes committed against humanity, but he said it was crucial for us to forgive the Germany that now existed—the country that had evolved into a civilized nation. "With forgiveness," he would say, "comes good health."

My father believed that anger, rage, resentment, and unforgiveness bred disease of the soul as well as the body. "Forgiveness," he told me, "is good medicine."

Years later, after having established my medical practice, my father and I had the opportunity to discuss forgiveness at length. I told him that I agreed with his philosophy and had found that anger and unforgiveness can truly eat away at the body and soul.

I recalled a patient who had told me that she was estranged from her two siblings because they had abandoned her in a time of need many years earlier. Although they all lived in the same small community, they were at odds with each other. As a result, my patient lived with anger, frustration, resentment, and a lack of forgiveness.

It was during an unrevealing and totally negative workup for abdominal pain, headaches, and high blood pressure that we talked about her situation. I told her of my father and how he had been able to forgive the unforgivable because he felt that without forgiveness, disease would pervade the body.

I expressed the opinion that her ailments could be partly attributed to her estrangement from her loved ones, and I urged my patient to consider reconciling with her family and to forgive them. Whatever it was they had done, it could not compare with what the Nazis had done to my parents and others.

Several years later, I received a letter from this woman, thanking me for that advice. She told me that she'd resolved the conflict with her sisters, and soon thereafter, her pain, headaches, and high blood pressure had abated. She had found forgiveness . . . and from this, good health.

I was therefore pleased to read a study published in the *American Journal of Cardiology* in August of 1992 that supported my father's sage advice. Stanford University researchers found that there was a direct correlation between anger and unhealthy changes in heart function.

The authors of this study stated that their findings seemed to offer a missing link between earlier studies, which revealed that people who were hostile by nature were five times more likely to die at an early age than those who were considered even-tempered. The authors recommended that people resolve their anger issues so as to improve their health.

So yes, I do believe that forgiveness can be very good medicine.

❀ ❀ ❀

Attitude As R$_x$

MY PARENTS HAD A FRIEND who worried about everything.

If she was healthy and feeling well, she believed that this state of good health wouldn't last long, so she would always answer the question of how she was doing with a curt, "Not bad, considering, but just wait, soon things will change." To her, it was bad luck to claim good health or good fortune.

As a child, I can still remember my parents advising this woman, "Don't worry so much." A hit song a few years ago echoed this same concept: "Don't Worry, Be Happy." This title seemed like good common sense to me. What's interesting is that scientists are increasingly finding that this "don't worry, be happy" idea is *more* that just good common sense—it's good medicine as well.

Researchers have found that individuals who worry a lot or who suppress their emotions show an accelerated heart rate and increased blood pressure while performing stress tests, as opposed to those who are emotionally healthy.

In addition, scientists who have followed medical students over 25 years noted that 14 percent of those students who had tested on the hostile and angry end of the test scale had died by the age of 50, while only 2 percent of those who were determined to be easygoing and even-tempered had died by that same age.

Stress, anger, worry, and depression result in a chronic and spasmodic outpouring of adrenaline in the body. This hormone, along with other related compounds also released during stressful times, act as poisons on the heart and cardiovascular system, leading to unhealthy conditions often associated with heart attacks and strokes.

On the other hand, a natural state of euphoria seems to protect the body against some of these adverse cardiovascular effects. Laughter, for example, has been noted to result in upper-body muscle tightening; and increased heart rate, blood pressure, and respiration, immediately followed by a healthy lowering of all of these parameters once the laughter has subsided.

William F. Frye, a Stanford University Medical Center psychiatrist and an expert on the subject of laughter, remarked on this beneficial effect of laughter by saying that "100 laughs is equivalent to ten minutes of rowing."

Suppressing one's problems does not seem to be beneficial to health, either. Constantly anxious or depressed individuals often present themselves to physicians with complaints of unexplained headaches and chest or abdominal pains resulting in expensive, time-consuming, and all too often, unnecessary, testing.

A behavioral medical research scientist at Duke University, Dr. Redford Williams, concluded that a link between stress and heart disease was plausible and was consistent with previous research linking heart disease to a lack of social support, hostility, and job strain.

So, attempting to minimize worry and stress should be a goal in all our lives. Helping us to achieve this aim should, therefore, be a top priority for medical professionals. While there are many ways in which organized medicine can help in this regard, I would suggest that physicians stop opening new medical centers . . . and begin opening comedy stores.

An Only Child

NOT HAVING HAD BROTHERS OR SISTERS, I have often wondered, *What is so awful about being an only child?*

Ask most couples how many children they want to have and you will rarely hear, "Just one." In fact, a recent survey showed that only 10 percent of Americans think that a one-child family is ideal. With the exception of the Chinese who, due to overpopulation, promote the one-child-per-family concept, most cultures put a premium on large families.

Since I make my living delivering babies, I'm certainly not averse to such attitudes. However, I do question why so many people believe that an only child might end up being mal-adjusted in some way.

Studies have revealed quite the opposite. It has been shown that an only child is more socially sensitive; does better in school; and is no more likely to be shy, self-centered, or spoiled than a child with siblings. In addition, these children are generally quite stable, secure, happy individuals.

Not having to share love and attention with siblings can result in a certain amount of stability and security, and since toys and playthings are not constantly being taken away by siblings, these kids find it easier to share with others when the need arises.

Other studies have confirmed that because they have an increased exposure to adults, only children have more expansive vocabularies and tend to mature earlier.

Of course, there are certain drawbacks to being an only child.

Unlike children from larger families who experience interaction with siblings on a daily basis, only children are often naive as to what is involved in developing and maintaining close family relationships.

Being an only child also places the responsibility of caring for aging parents squarely on our shoulders. We alone function as our parents' support system. While we do not have to share in the process of dividing assets upon our parents' deaths, we do miss the nurturing support of siblings when we lose those special parental relationships. We cry alone when those who brought us into the world depart this Earth.

Nonetheless, as couples decide on the number of children to bring into the world, it seems important to ask whether they have considered if one child may, in fact, be enough.

I have taken care of chronically ill patients who, having struggled through the hazards of bearing one child, actually decide to plan for a second child merely because their concept of family includes another son or daughter. They ignore the argument that there is nothing wrong with raising one child and that, in fact, an only child may enjoy economic opportunities not always available to others.

Perhaps couples planning their childbearing future should ask themselves an important question before embarking on the journey of parenthood: *What is so awful about being an only child?*

Positive Parenting: The Easiest Part

MANY PEOPLE WOULD AGREE that parenting is one of the most difficult tasks that human beings can undertake. Yet it has always amazed me how ill prepared we are to perform our role as parents competently.

While there are hundreds of books and plenty of advice from experts on the subject, most of us learn the art of being parents as we go along, much as our parents did with us. No single theory fits all situations, and certainly, there is little agreement on how to be an effective parent. However, having practiced obstetrics for many years and having witnessed interactions between thousands of parents and their children, I have come to certain conclusions.

First, I'd like to point out that the single most important physiological act that a baby performs upon being born is to replace its water-filled lungs with air. It does so by crying. The louder and harder the cry, the better we health-care providers in the delivery room feel. Yet time after time, this normal occurrence has been interpreted by parents as the newborn being angry or upset. "He's going to be a mean one," are words I've heard all too often. A persistently crying baby at home has resulted in similar parental reaction: "Don't pick him up or we'll spoil him." This is nonsense!

Babies are not born angry—they learn that emotion later in life. A newborn cries because he or she is hungry, wet, uncomfortable, bored, or seeking human contact. By responding to this cry, parents are not spoiling the child, they are merely remedying the problem, as well as offering much-needed comfort and love.

But the most significant problem I see in the parenting area has to do with a parent's failure to help a child build self-confidence.

I grew up in a home with parents who told me how wonderful I was on a daily basis. No matter what I did, I was generally praised. My watercoloring was the best, my attempt at playing the clarinet was unsurpassed, as were my awkward dives into the swimming pool (no matter that in all these endeavors, I was well below average). The important thing was that I was instilled with confidence by the two people who had the most contact with me during my formative years.

If children are told how wonderful they are every day, eventually they begin to believe it. It is this type of confidence that can propel a child to success in any area—and help create a secure and happy adult.

All too often, I have seen parents fail to compliment their child at a vulnerable time, and I have also witnessed parents openly criticizing their child after his or her genuine attempt to please. For some parents, nothing that their child does is good enough.

How sad it is to witness a child's crushed reaction to such parental criticism. As parents, it is our responsibility to help our children build confidence in themselves. And we have the means to do so with a simple word of praise. We must get this message out to everyone involved in parenting, as well as to potential parents.

The future of our children depends on it.

Can We Talk?

As JOAN RIVERS OFTEN SAYS, "Can we talk?" My daughter has just turned 14, and I'm concerned.

As an obstetrician/gynecologist, I am acutely aware of the problems caused by teenage sexual experimentation, so I'm worried about how my daughter and I are going to survive these turbulent years.

I know, for example, that by the end of the ninth grade, 30 percent of teenagers in this country will have had sexual intercourse, and that by graduation, that figure hits 70 percent.

I'm also aware that there are close to a million cases of HIV-infected individuals in this country, with a 44 percent increase among heterosexuals over the past five years, making our teenagers vulnerable to this deadly virus. And I know a lot more.

Sexually transmitted diseases, including gonorrhea, infect three million teenagers each year. In addition, 500,000 new cases of herpes, 4 million new cases of chlamydia, and 24 million new cases of human papilloma virus occur every year, with high prevalence rates among teens.

To make matters worse, I know that because they're used inconsistently—if at all—condoms, which are now readily available to all teens, often fail to protect our children from these diseases, as well as from unwanted pregnancies.

Each year, approximately one million teenagers get pregnant, with 400,000 choosing abortion. The rest begin their lives bearing the significant burdens of early parenthood, thereby robbing them of so much of the fun, education, adventure, and personal growth they could be experiencing as young adults.

There's more.

When questioned after the fact, the majority of teenage girls report that they wish they had waited to have sex, that it wasn't satisfying at all, and that they only did it because of intense peer and boyfriend pressure.

Barbara Whitehead, writing in the *Atlantic Monthly,* said that sex among teenagers tends to be "nasty, brutish, and short."

What really troubles me, though, is the fact that despite pervasive sexual education for teens in our school system, the data indicates that it is just not working very well. Teenagers may know more about sex overall in a technical sense, but they're still under considerable pressure to have unprotected and frequent sexual intercourse.

Much of the content of sex education courses is based on facts rather than on a value-based information system. Minimal effort is geared toward helping teenagers learn to say no and mean it. Most young girls tell pollsters that they would have liked more help in saying no without hurting a boy's feelings. Little emphasis is placed on teaching both sexes that abstinence and virginity are positive virtues.

In a society that is bombarded by sexual innuendoes on television, in movies, and in books and magazines; and with an educational system that approaches subjects such as safe sex in an inadequate way, it's little wonder that our kids find themselves doing things that often result in severe, lifelong, physical and emotional scars.

I'm not advocating the abolishment of sex education for teenagers. I would just like these courses to place more emphasis on the virtue of virginity, at least until our young people reach an age where they can handle the emotional and physical consequence in a responsible manner.

In particular, I want these courses to advocate the art of saying no. That doesn't mean I'm blind to the fact that teenagers will experiment with sex, but why does "going all the way" have to be an integral part of our teens' lives?

I want so much to tell my daughter all these things.

I want to tell her to wait, and to be firm in withstanding peer pressure. I want to tell her that maintaining virginity throughout these tough teenage years is really important, and that someday she'll be glad that she followed this advice. But how do I impress all this upon her and at the same time assure her that if she finds herself in trouble, she can still turn to me for help?

How do I do all this when I know that she would rather choose being grounded from going to the mall with her friends for a year than talk about such things with her father?

Perhaps I will suggest that she read this essay.

Waiting-Room Blues

NOT TOO LONG AGO, I found myself sitting in a doctor's office as a patient. Being a physician, it was beneficial for me to be on the other end of the doctor/patient relationship, as it made me more aware of a dilemma that exists throughout the medical profession.

That problem has to do with the waiting period from the scheduled appointment time to actual visitation time with the physician. There is no doubt about it—many people have to wait interminable periods before actually seeing their doctor, causing significant frustration and irritation.

However, there's more to this subject than perhaps one might realize. To best explain this, I need to go back many years to the beginning of my private practice, which I had established in my hometown after seven years of training following medical school.

I was 32 years old and anxious to get started. At first, my waiting room was often empty and my patient load light. For those few patients who did make appointments, I found myself sitting down with them right on time and discussing many aspects of their medical care for extended periods.

Those early patients apparently went home and told their friends that not only did I see them on time, but they received a lot of attention during their visit. Thus, my practice grew. However, I found that as the number of patients increased, although I was still seeing them with almost no waiting period, I had to lessen our time together.

Still, the number of patients grew. In an effort to handle this situation, I extended my office hours. Finally, as happens to most young physicians, I reached a point where I had to make a decision: Should I insist on seeing patients on time and thereby shorten even further the time spent with them, or would I allow for an increased waiting time yet assure that my patients all received the attention they deserved?

I chose the latter. I set up my practice so that once patients were seen, they would leave my office feeling that they had spent enough time with me to get their questions answered and their medical needs met. That was my ultimate goal.

My practice continued to grow, and my duties and responsibilities expanded. Emergency deliveries, surgeries, and other procedures were added to my patient load, and I was finding it increasingly difficult to keep the waiting time reasonable.

To maintain control over this seemingly out-of-control situation, I informed my secretary that she would have to limit the number of patients I saw. However, in spite of this attempt at streamlining things, my secretary kept coming to me to tell me of a patient who was a friend of a friend, or a relative of a relative, or wife or daughter of a colleague—or just someone who really needed my help.

What could I do? Many of my patients were now waiting 30 to 60 minutes to see me. I was frustrated, and so were they. My choices were becoming more and more limited. In addition, I found myself feeling guilty during office hours, knowing that my patients were waiting so long. I felt that I was letting them down, adding to their already overburdened lives.

Despite what you may think, chances are that your doctor is just as upset at having to *make* you wait as you are frustrated by *having* to wait. In my case, all I could do was make sure that once patients and I met face-to-face, I gave them the very best medical care possible and helped them feel that it was all worth it.

Although doctors can reduce their patient load somewhat, the modern economics of medicine come into play. Before even opening the door of an office, physicians are saddled with huge medical malpractice fees. Add to this the cost of office space, secretarial support, equipment, and nurses, and it is understandable that doctors must either continue to see as many patients as possible, or raise fees for those who *are* seen. Insurance companies and managed-care groups, however, make this latter option impossible since they refuse to cover additional charges.

In all fairness, medical care cannot be compared to other lines of work. Matters of life and death and good physical and mental health are at stake, and are not comparable to taking a car to the shop or a financial problem to an accountant.

So as I sat waiting for my own physician, the clock ticking away, I was glad I had freed up the next few hours. I knew that the wait meant that my doctor was handling the needs of another patient who needed his assistance.

It was then I realized that . . . doctors wait, too.

Childless Heartbreak

There are infertility specialists who—no pun intended—maintain that infertility is inconceivable. Well, I can tell you that infertility is *very* conceivable.

My wife, Julie, and I spent five years trying to bring a child of our own into this world. Although we were unsuccessful in our attempts, we were able to reconcile this fact and get on with our lives.

However, this childless state of ours did not evolve without a fight. A thorough infertility workup with painful tests, complicated surgery, numerous medications, and three in-vitro fertilization (IVF) attempts resulted in four heart-wrenching miscarriages and considerable out-of-pocket expense.

Because we've gone through this difficult yet unsuccessful process, we are both very sensitive to the many claims made by those in the fertility field to "cure infertility." Based on information gathered from infertility experts, the media generally paints a very rosy picture for infertile couples, reporting seemingly endless stories of successful pregnancies achieved through a variety of sophisticated, complicated, and expensive reproductive technologies.

Yet, few stories portray the reality and the plight of those couples who are not successful in becoming parents. Despite what you have read or seen, such people constitute a rather large group.

I believe that the stories relating to unsuccessful attempts are also important to tell. Couples need to be made aware that they may not end up with a live birth, and must be prepared to deal with the fact that they may be forever childless (unless they adopt). This is a very difficult and painful realization.

Infertility affects approximately 15 percent of couples attempting to get pregnant. In the over-35-year-old group, that figure is doubled. Among these individuals, approximately 80 percent can be helped with some simple remedies, while the rest are put through much more complicated reproductive processes such as IVF—also known as the test-tube baby process, where a woman's egg is fertilized outside the body and then the embryo is inserted into her uterus. Getting pregnant through IVF is said to occur as much as 40 percent of the time. Yet, a truly successful outcome of pregnancy through IVF is one that results in a live birth. This occurs *only 25 percent* of the time for each IVF attempt.

This means that three out of four couples are unsuccessful after an IVF procedure. Multiple cycles may improve this percentage somewhat; however, many couples still remain childless.

Childless couples often have a difficult time coping in a society where kids seem to be everywhere. A husband and wife who can't have children and choose not to adopt go through challenging times as they try to adjust to life without kids of their own. Since there are so many couples who find themselves in this situation—even after extensive infertility treatments—it is crucial for people to know the facts and understand the limitations.

There *is* life after infertility, however, and it's important that couples acknowledge this and get on with their lives in a productive, meaningful, and fulfilling way. There has to be a time during the lengthy process of infertility testing, treatment, and failure when a couple says, "Enough!" Enough pain, enough heartache, enough anguish and disappointment.

Reaching that point comes at a different time for each couple, yet eventually it *must* come. When the truth of the matter is finally accepted, couples can know in their hearts and minds that they did everything . . . conceivable . . . and that a life without children is anything but meaningless.

It is still a life filled with purpose and love.

❧ ❧ ❧

The Joys of Growing Older

I HAVE NEVER UNDERSTOOD why so many people (especially women) over the age of 40 are reluctant to reveal their age. Is it because they're afraid to admit that they're growing older? Or is it because they're afraid of being judged in a certain way as soon as they state their "number"? Well, whatever the case, Americans are getting older, and I think we'd better accept that fact.

While the average life expectancy in the United States is now 76.3 years, in 55 years it will be 82.6 years. Thirteen percent (34 million) of the 281 million Americans living in the U.S. are 65 years or older, and that figure will hit 20 percent (that's one American in every five) by the year 2050. In addition, the proportion of American citizens age 85 or older is growing rapidly. Three million are age 85 or older, and that number will climb to 19 million by the year 2050.

I happen to enjoy the benefits growing older. Granted, the best reason for appreciating my increasing age is the alternative. Yet, there are other compelling and reasonable arguments that can be made to convince others of the joy of aging.

First, age brings wisdom. Living into one's elder years allows one to experience the richness and fullness of life, and to learn many valuable lessons. As we grow older, we're better equipped to know what we want and what we don't want. Hopefully, we can avoid making the same mistakes we did when we were younger, and use the time we do have more wisely.

We may also find ourselves in more stable, nurturing relationships with friends and family. It finally dawns on us as we age that the people who have been in our lives for so many years are really worth treasuring. As we grow older, we nurture those friendships more, and derive myriad benefits from such enduring relationships.

Similarly, we tend to look more lovingly upon our family members, who have been by our side through numerous joys and crises. We appreciate them to a greater extent and are more apt to express our heartfelt feelings to them.

We are also able to relax more, because we don't take things quite so seriously anymore. We take the time to smell flowers, feel the wind at our backs, watch the sun rise and set—and are simply more aware of our overall surroundings.

Growing *up* is fun, but so is growing *older*. I look forward to this continuous, fascinating process called aging.

After all, aging is inevitable, so why not relax and enjoy it?

Are You Somebody?

EVER SINCE I WAS A YOUNG BOY, movies have fascinated me.

Being raised at a time when radio served the purpose that TV does today, going to the movies was probably the most exciting activity in my life. Even with the advent of television, I still maintained an avid interest in movies and the actors and actresses who appeared in them.

So it was with great anticipation and excitement that I accepted an invitation from friends to attend the 1991 Academy Awards presentation in Hollywood. Not only were my wife and I invited to the awards show, but we were also to be driven to this gala event in a limousine and then attend a post-awards party. I felt like a kid who knows he's going to visit Disneyland for the first time.

Dressed in black tie and sporting my often-worn black Stetson hat, I helped my wife into a well-equipped limousine that took us from our hotel in L.A. to the Shrine Auditorium. Following a long line of limousines (800 in all, I was told), we traveled the final half-mile while gaping at screaming fans on either side of the road.

Upon emerging from the limousine, we were momentarily blinded by the bright lights and flashing cameras. Arriving in between Jon Bon Jovi and Jeff Bridges, we were literally in a swirl of excitement, with television cameras, paparazzi, and commentators straining to make their way through the throng.

Although we knew that none of this hubbub had anything to do with us, we nonetheless realized that this was an experience that would probably never be repeated in our lives, and accordingly, we smiled and waved to the cameras with enthusiasm. For a fleeting moment, we felt as if we were true Hollywood stars.

What followed is best described as a trip down the "yellow brick road" of Hollywood fantasy. Saying hello to Al Pacino, having Jeremy Irons kiss my wife's hand when she wished him good luck, and standing next to such personalities as Sophia Loren, Julia Roberts, Robert DeNiro, and Richard Gere created a surrealistic atmosphere.

The party that followed this grand evening was held in a nearby restaurant. Attendees included actors such as Susan Sarandon, Christopher Reeve, and the man who played "Miles" on the once-popular TV show *thirtysomething*.

Standing alone momentarily, sipping champagne, I gazed around the room. It was exactly what you'd expect from a star-studded Hollywood party—there were beautiful women and handsome men laughing, dancing, drinking, and making small talk while they themselves also scanned the room for familiar celebrity faces.

Suddenly a woman stepped to my side, and with pen and paper in hand, she asked a question that caught me off-guard for a second. "I'm with *People* magazine," she said. "Are you somebody?"

I guess it was the party, the tuxedo, and the big hat that confused this uninformed reporter as she struggled to determine if I was worth talking to. It was then that I realized how surreal this entire evening had been and how superficial the Tinseltown mentality really was. It symbolized appearances, celluloid moments, and facades, while elevating the entertainment personality to unrealistic and exaggerated levels.

For a moment, I almost felt disappointed that I was just a doctor from Tennessee and not "somebody." Quickly regaining my composure, however, I remembered that of course I was somebody. We are *all* somebody—whether doctor, farmer, laborer, salesman, or housewife. How sad for anyone to even ask such a question. And so I informed the reporter that, of course I was somebody and would be glad to grant her an interview.

Somewhat taken aback by my response, she smiled, stepped back ever so cautiously, and disappeared into the crowd. I realized that I had been given a reminder that evening about what's truly important in life and what's not—and to think that it took a trip to Hollywood and the Academy Awards to get it.

A Way Out of Hell

MY NEW PATIENT'S STORY of her first pregnancy was indeed tragic.

Within weeks of delivering her first child, a healthy baby girl, this new mother had become severely depressed, eventually requiring prolonged hospitalization, heavy doses of medication, and psychotherapy. Although she had been symptom free for the past year, she was pregnant once more. Fearful of falling into a depression again, she sought my medical opinion and advice.

I started our discussion by offering a few facts. I told her that depression was a serious mood disorder attacking the mind as well as the body. I also told her it was relatively common.

Approximately 17 million Americans are believed to suffer from clinical depression each year, with only about half seeking treatment. While it has been estimated that one out of every five adults suffers from depression at some time in their lives, twice as many of these people are women, and a large number are women in their reproductive years.

I told my patient that, while there is still much to be learned about depression, scientists believe that it is probably caused by an imbalance of chemicals in the brain that carry communication between nerve cells that control our mood. I also informed her that although many years ago there was no real treatment for this ailment, today many new medications exist that affect brain chemistry, thus alleviating many of the symptoms of depression.

I also comforted her by explaining that in many cases such as hers, these new medications would have a real chance of preventing a reoccurrence of her depression after delivery of her child. To say the least, she was relieved to hear that there was something the medical profession had to offer her to prevent the hell she had experienced many years ago.

❖ ❖ ❖

Clinical depression is a serious illness. While most of us experience "the blues" occasionally, real chemical depression cannot be willed away. Without treatment, symptoms can last for months, or even years.

Typical symptoms include a depressed mood; a diminished interest in activities that were once enjoyed; changes in appetite and sleep habits; loss of energy; lack of concentration; a feeling of helplessness, worthlessness and guilt; and even thoughts of suicide. In fact, it is estimated that 30,000 people each year take their own lives due to depression. Depression is more common in women, yet the male-to-female suicide rate is four-to-one. The common myth that suicide is the reaction to a life crisis, teenage turmoil, or advanced aging is inaccurate. Suicide is generally indicative of a severe, underlying depression that can often be successfully treated.

Interestingly, scientists are discovering that, as is the case with many other conditions, depression is more common in certain individuals. A previous episode, a family history, being female, and the postpartum state are common risk factors.

What the general public may not know is that there are several different types of this condition, such as major depression, dysthymia, bipolar disorder, and seasonal depression. Physicians treat each type somewhat differently.

Seasonal affective disorder, for example, occurs in the winter months and recedes in the spring and summer. Psychiatrists tell us that it is the absence of sunlight that triggers a biochemical reaction causing this type of depression, which is found much more commonly in women and children. It is treated, in part, by therapy that includes exposure to intense light for a period of time each day. It should be noted that seasonal affective disorder should not be confused with the very common winter "holiday blues."

It's encouraging to know that clinical depression can be alleviated, with eight out of ten individuals responding successfully to treatment such as medication and psychotherapy by the end of one year. Newer medications that have been developed in the past few years have truly revolutionized the treatment of clinical depression.

As far as my patient was concerned, her pregnancy progressed without problems. Her mood was generally upbeat and positive, but on the first day following delivery of her second little girl, I put her on depression medication as a preventive measure.

Returning to my office every two weeks so that I could review her situation, my patient remained happy and excited about her new baby and life in general. The dark hole of depression that had once invaded her life never returned.

Planning Each Day

ABY WARBURG, AN EARLY 20TH-CENTURY art critic and member of the famous Warburg banking family, was once quoted as saying, "Plan each day as if you were going to live forever, and live each day as if you were going to die by day's end."

While reflecting on this meaningful quote, it occurred to me that many Americans plan and live their lives in the exact opposite fashion. Most live each day as if they're going to live forever, and plan each day as if they're going to die by day's end. It appears that Americans generally believe they can live each day without a care for tomorrow—as if what they do will not effect their longevity.

For example, statistics show that one-third of all Americans are overweight. There is more fat in our diet today than ever before, despite all the low-fat foods on grocery shelves and the knowledge that a high-fat diet is dangerous to our health. Thirty percent of Americans smoke, in spite of the well-documented list of serious consequences, such as lung cancer, emphysema, and low birth weight in newborns.

Only 40 percent of us do any form of regular physical exercise, making the remaining 60 percent of Americans "couch potatoes." This is the case despite overwhelming evidence that regular exercise can reduce heart disease, as well as make us feel better about ourselves emotionally and physically.

We drink too much alcohol, drive our cars too fast, refuse to buckle our seat belts, and neglect getting annual medical checkups. In addition, we buy too much on credit, save less money than others in industrialized countries, and don't seriously consider our days of retirement. In other words, we do very little to ensure that we'll have long, healthy, productive lives.

On the other hand, we often plan our days as if it might be our last! We purchase day planners in the form of computers and calendars, pagers, cellular phones, and the like—

regimenting, organizing, and structuring our daily lives at the expense of spontaneity and joy.

While some planning at work is important, we have gone too far in our desire to control our day-to-day activities, and we have extended this planning to include recreational activities as well. We run on autopilot through our days, without any thought other than the task before us—similar to those car rides along familiar roadways, where we realize we've arrived at our destination, but are unable to remember the drive itself.

We neglect to smell flowers, taste flavors, feel textures, sense the wind, or witness the sun rising and setting. How often do we stop and reflect on how lucky we are to be on this planet and to be a part of the incredible experience of life? Even when we're ostensibly relaxing at home, our lives often seem too structured and regimented. No wonder Americans are fatigued and need a vacation . . . when they return home from their vacation.

Warburg was right. We should plan each day as if we're going to live forever, and live each day as if it were our last. By doing so, although we may not live forever, each day will be treated as the precious gem that it truly is.

No Need to Panic

AN ARTICLE THAT I READ in the newspaper on anxiety disorders caught my attention. It stated that this affliction affects 12 percent of adults in the United States (about 23 million) at some point in their lives.

I thought back to my second year in medical school when I was one of those 23 million. Things were different then, however, and no one in the medical profession seemed to know how to help me.

Working and studying at a furious, never-ending pace, that year became overwhelming for me. Holding down several part-time jobs and finding it necessary to study long into the night each day of the week, I was steadily becoming more and more frustrated, lonely, and unhappy. While my non-medical student friends were seemingly enjoying active social lives with plenty of leisure time, my life seemed empty and overbearing.

Initially, I noticed that I was having difficulty sleeping. Then one day while sitting in class, I noticed that my heart was pounding rapidly. When the overhead lights were turned off to allow the professor to show slides, I experienced a feeling of panic. I could not sit still and had to exit through a side door to catch my breath and attempt to calm the feelings overwhelming my 23-year-old body.

I could not concentrate or study, and my grades were suffering. I was becoming concerned that whatever was happening to me was serious and might prevent me from obtaining a medical degree.

Not understanding my symptoms, I sought medical care from a variety of physicians in town. Despite an extensive in-hospital workup for adrenal tumors, diabetes, cardiac disease, and cancer, none of the experts could determine what was wrong with me.

Requesting and receiving a two-week medical leave of absence from school, I went home. Alarmed by my condition, my mother attempted to nurse me back to health. From holding me in her arms while I tried to fall asleep in my well-lit room at night, to feeding me copious amounts of my favorite foods, my loving mother tried everything she could think of, but she could not alter my "condition."

Suddenly and dramatically during my second week at home, a breakthrough occurred. Totally frustrated and worried, my mother gave me one of her tranquilizers called Miltown. During the early '60s, Miltown was one of the first of a class of tranquilizers soon to be replaced by dozens of other more effective medications. Keeping a few pills in her medicine cabinet to use for occasional stress, my mother was willing to try anything in the hopes that something would help.

How right she was. Within 72 hours of taking this medication, I was cured—back in school and functioning normally.

❧ ❧ ❧

Anxiety disorders include phobia and obsessive/compulsive behavior, as well as what I had—panic disorder—and are the most prevalent forms of mental illness. They are also among the most expensive, having cost this country approximately $47 million in 1990. Seventy-five percent of those costs were indirect and included lost productivity, absenteeism, and disability. The remaining 25 percent stemmed from more direct costs including medication, hospitalization, and physician care.

The article on anxiety disorder that caught my attention noted that because of the stigma associated with mental illness, and inadequate training that prevents doctors from making the proper diagnosis, only about one-third of individuals with these disorders receives treatment.

A Clue to Cancer

I FIRST HEARD ABOUT THE DISCOVERY of the BRCA1 gene in the same way that almost everyone else in this country did: I read about it in the newspaper.

BRCA1 is a gene that suppresses tumor growth in such organs as the breast, ovary, colon, and prostate gland, and if altered by a mutation, will result in a very high incidence of cancer in that individual whose BRCA1 does not work properly. It has been estimated that a woman who has a defective BRCA1 gene has a 94 percent chance of developing cancer of the breast or ovary by the age of 70.

Imagine, then, my interest and concern when I read about the discovery of BRCA1. My wife's family history is riddled with stories of cancer, including a father who died of colon cancer, and a mother and aunt who died of breast cancer. In addition, there are other related family members inflicted with malignant disease.

For just a brief moment, I wondered whether or not I should tell my wife about this test. Should I go along with the old notion that ignorance is bliss and not burden her with this news?

Of course, I quickly realized that this information might play a key role in someday saving her life. If she possessed an abnormality in her BRCA1 gene, she could consider a number of options, including frequent mammograms and a possible bilateral prophylactic mastectomy (which would reduce her chance of developing breast cancer dramatically), removal of her ovaries (which would effectively eliminate any chance of developing ovarian cancer), and frequent colon exams.

However, we would also have to consider the insurance ramifications. If she tested positive, would we be required to place this information in her medical records and thereby risk her losing her health insurance someday?

After discussing these issues, my wife and I decided to explore our options. First, I called the University of Pennsylvania, whose lab was running this test, and spoke to the woman in charge of the counseling and testing program. She was very helpful and informed me that we would first have to see a genetic counselor at Vanderbilt. Our counselor would obtain a family history called a pedigree and send it to the University of Pennsylvania. If my wife was considered to be at a high risk for carrying a mutant BRCA1 gene, then they would contact us and request a blood sample.

We obtained the required genetic counseling and decided to enter the program. We then sent the pedigree to Pennsylvania and did what so many others do after medical tests . . . we waited.

The waiting seemed interminable. During that time, we discussed how we would respond if the test turned out to be positive. We also talked about what we would do if it were negative. The BRCA1 gene is only a cause of 5 percent of all breast cancers, so we still had to consider our options even if the test showed no evidence of a mutant gene.

Finally, weeks after our initial counseling session, we were informed that, yes, the University of Pennsylvania believed my wife's history was strong enough to be included in their research protocol, and that we should now send her blood to their lab for testing.

Somewhat relieved, we did as they told us, and along with enclosing a considerable fee, we dropped the package with its precious cargo in the mail. This time they told us that the testing would take four to six months, and that as soon as the testing was finished and the results known, our genetic counselor at Vanderbilt would have us return for a face-to-face counseling session to fully explain the results, positive or negative.

And so once again, we waited.

This time, however, the level of anxiety was much higher and more intense. One month felt like three, and two months like six. Despite my background in medicine, I was worried about how we would handle this information, especially since we both believed that considering my wife's history, she would more than likely turn out to have a positive test.

The day finally arrived when we heard the genetic counselor's voice at the other end of the line, ending the waiting period. The results were in. Could we come to her office that next week to discuss the findings?

Of course we could, and the date was set. We once again did what we had done several times before—we waited. We would now have an answer, and regardless of the result, we knew we had made the correct decision to be tested. As medical science continues to develop new genetic tests that may determine and affect our fate in life, we may all be confronted with the need to make similar decisions.

The benefits of knowing—especially if we are able to alter the outcome— clearly seem to outweigh the negative consequences of not knowing.

As Old As You Feel

YOU KNOW THAT OLD SAYING: "You're only as old as you feel"? Well, that's only partly true. I believe that you're also as old as you *think*.

I came to that conclusion last April on my birthday as I walked along a sunny beach in Florida. My birthday usually finds me in a pensive, reflective, and contemplative mood, so it was natural for me to begin thinking about the fact that at the age of 56, I was slowly, but surely, heading toward what many call old age.

But exactly how would I know when I had reached this milestone in life?

If I was truly as old as I felt, then on this particular day, I *felt* 56 years old. My muscles had been increasingly stiff in the mornings, and my joints periodically ached. My back was causing me considerable problems, and spicy foods were no longer agreeing with me. I woke up several times during the night, felt fatigued in the latter parts of the day, and frequently found that I had little stamina for late-evening activities. And, just like my father had when he hit his mid-50s, I was experiencing that ever-so-familiar abdominal bulge, despite exercising and watching what I ate.

Yet, despite feeling 56 physically, my brain kept telling me I was only 35, and this was causing problems for me.

For example, thinking I was in my 30s, I thought nothing about challenging a high school friend of my daughter, who was on the track team, to a 100-yard dash. Since I had run this event in high school, I believed I could at least hold my own and maybe even impress my daughter. Embarrassment was more the result! At about 80 yards into the race, and with my opponent yards ahead of me, I tore my left hamstring muscles and spent weeks in rest and rehabilitation.

Another time, knowing that I was in shape and thinking I was invincible, I didn't hesitate to run five miles on Saturday and three miles early Sunday morning, followed by a competitive game of racquetball with a friend on Sunday afternoon. Into the third game, my fatigued muscles took over, causing me to fall and tear my Achilles tendon. This resulted in surgery; and six months of a cast, crutches, and rehabilitation.

There's more.

Despite feeling increasing back pain while jogging, I just could not accept the fact that my running days were coming to an end—until one day after a particularly long run, I couldn't get out of bed for three days. I was *thinking* 35, but I was *feeling* 56.

And so, on that birthday walk last year, I made a resolution. I would try very hard to let my body tell my brain what it could do, rather than the other way around. I actually put into practice what I tell so many of my patients to do: I *listened* to my body.

Instead of jogging, I took up walking. Instead of racquetball, I began playing tennis because I found it easier on my stamina and joints. And instead of a winter ski trip to Aspen, it was off to the beach. I gave up eating spicy foods and added a 15-minute nap to my afternoon routine.

My 56th year came and went, and I found myself walking down that same stretch of beach recently on my 57th birthday. I realized that my new strategy had indeed worked. While I still *thought* younger than I felt, I *felt* much better thinking smart.

Being an Orphan

The dictionary defines an orphan as a child whose parents are dead. After all these years, I realize that I am no longer someone's child. I am an orphan.

I became an orphan after my mother died in 1991. Although my father had died three years earlier, my mother's death left me with a different kind of loneliness, a feeling that I had not experienced before, and was having a hard time understanding.

Not long after the funeral, I visited my parents' grave site one mild and beautiful autumn day. As I sat under a tree near where my beloved parents were laid to rest, I sensed that the unique type of loneliness I was feeling was probably similar to that of a young child whose parents had died. I longed to see and be with my mom and dad. I wanted to hug them and kiss them and tell them all the wonderful things that were happening in my life. But of course I couldn't.

Fortunately, I was extremely blessed because my mother-in-law, Dorothy, filled a great deal of the void left by my parents' passing. We were very close and maintained a loving relationship very much like mother and son. However, when Dorothy died, that feeling of "orphanhood" came rushing forth in even greater waves.

Because losing Dorothy also made my wife, Julie, an orphan, we were able to go through this lonely feeling together. Seeing our friends, or even perfect strangers, interact with one or more of their parents brought a knowing look into our eyes, and a shared sense of loss. Certain TV commercials or movies depicting adults lovingly interacting with a parent brought moisture to our eyes as well.

Both of us have noted how often we have wanted to pick up the phone and dial that familiar number to our parents' homes, just to hear their voices or to ask a question that we failed to ask while they were alive. Also, our parents' birthdays and anniversaries always inspire us to think private, loving thoughts of special times once celebrated, but photos and memories are now all that remain.

And then there are the holidays.

It is during these days in particular that the feeling of orphanhood really comes crashing down. Although I am very blessed to have children and other family members to share these times with, I rarely experience a holiday or special occasion that isn't somewhat bittersweet.

Our society is very much parent and child oriented: from Mother's Day and Father's Day, to mother-daughter teas and father-son outings, we are constantly reminded of the loved ones we no longer have.

Orphanhood, like childhood, is just another rite of passage along life's path. Perhaps our society needs to be more sensitive to those who do not have mothers and fathers . . . and who are no longer someone's child.

Becoming More Aware

I MARVEL AT THE ABILITY OF HUMANS to properly function while being totally unaware of their surroundings.

I am referring specifically to that car ride home when you suddenly arrive at your destination and realize you don't remember the actual drive or any familiar landmarks passed.

Despite the fact that your mind was obviously off somewhere else, you were still able to send appropriate signals to arms, legs, and eyes to allow safe passage through heavy traffic, changing lights, and stop signs. Unfortunately, many of us too often go through our lives in this same robotic fashion. We work and play, yet we're not really aware of our surroundings or any real aspect of the experience itself. In other words, we often go through life much like that car ride, suddenly finding that life is over and that we haven't really been aware enough to live in the moment.

It's not that we have not been *advised* to be more aware. Go to the self-help section of any bookstore and you'll see that there are numerous books related to the subject of awareness. It isn't easy, however, to train oneself to become aware. It's a feat that must be practiced repeatedly before it can become a part of one's daily routine.

Many years ago, having finished a book entitled *Be Here Now,* I realized that I needed help to learn how to live in the here-and-now. Too often I found that I was cognizant of entering the hospital in the early morning and leaving later that night. I had acted like an automaton during the in-between periods and, therefore, had lost an important chunk of the day.

Thus, I began training myself to become more aware.

Each time I used my pocket watch to check the time, or when I merely felt it nestled in my pocket while going about my daily activities, I used this act to cause me to stop and initiate an awareness process. I thought about how I was feeling, what was happening, and in general, I made a point of noticing the many wonderful things that were taking place around me.

Years later, I was able to put aside my watch as a triggering process and enter this awareness phase spontaneously each day.

I think that many of us have difficulty living in the present. We glorify the past and look to the future to give us joy or peace. Katharine Graham, at the end of her book, *Personal History*, stated it well: "I am grateful to be able to go on working and to like my new life so well that I don't miss the old one. It is dangerous, when you are older, to start living in the past."

The good ol' days are happening now, not then. Winston Churchill, reflecting as a youth on the subject of life after death, also said it wisely: "People who think much of the next world rarely prosper in this."

Living for the future robs us of the value and worth of the present. I believe we can and should become more aware of each and every moment of our lives. We must awaken from our sleepwalking by sharpening our senses, really taking heed of all the beauty in our environment.

Time for My Nap

I HAVE A CONFESSION TO MAKE: I often need to take a nap to get through the day. So there, I've said it. I realize how this must sound, but wait before you pass judgment. Napping is a preventive health measure that our society should look at more closely.

I never wanted to take a nap as a young child when my mother used to insist upon it, but it's now something I do eagerly and voluntarily. I now realize that a daily nap was, and is, quite important.

For reasons I am not so sure of, Americans regard napping as something negative rather than positive. Perhaps it's because we're so work-oriented that taking time out of a busy day to rest and regroup is frowned upon, as if it implies laziness or lack of drive and motivation.

I see it the other way around. Napping is not only something beneficial, but it has the potential to increase productivity.

I did not always nap, mostly because it seemed like a luxury I couldn't afford. However, after I turned 50, I discovered two things: One, around mid-afternoon I would feel a soreness and tiredness creep through my body that actually slowed me down; and two, allowing myself a few minutes a day to nap was not a luxury, it was a necessity.

At first, I ignored the symptoms that accompany fatigue and struggled through the day. Then I began to simply put my feet up for 10 or 15 minutes in the afternoon and sensed a definite improvement. That routine soon developed into an actual snooze!

Waking up from my "nap," I found myself refreshed and rejuvenated, ready for both the remainder of the day, as well as a full evening of activities.

Some of you may be closet nappers—you grab a snooze here and there, but you don't tell anyone for fear of disapproval. It may interest you to know that many of the world's greatest men and women took (and still do take) daily naps. The great Winston Churchill was known to take afternoon naps; and so was Johannes Brahms, Napoleon Bonaparte, Stonewall Jackson, and Maxwell Taylor. Ronald Reagan and Bill Clinton are said to take naps as well. Entire countries routinely close their shops in the afternoon, have lunch, and take a siesta before reopening for business later in the day.

Taking an afternoon nap should be more accepted in our society, since it has been well documented that Americans are generally sleep deprived. Many myths surrounding napping create some of the reluctance to snooze.

There is the myth that napping interferes with nighttime sleep. It does not. Nor is the desire to nap a result of needing to rest after lunch. Sleepiness occurs whether one eats lunch or not.

Then there is the myth that taking an afternoon nap is abnormal. Clearly each of us has a biological rhythm. Included in that rhythm, for many of us, is the need to rest in the middle of the day. Studies have revealed that two out of three adults nap at least once a week, so it cannot be that abnormal.

There is an old saying that time is the most valuable thing that one can spend. No matter where you work or how you spend your time each day, perhaps you can find a way to announce to those around you: "Excuse me while I take a short nap." It might mean taking time out of your lunch hour to allow yourself a few minutes to put your feet up. Or it might mean skipping that afternoon coffee break to close your eyes for a few minutes. But whatever you do, you will find a new, rejuvenated person at the end of each day.

Perhaps we should all rethink how we use our breaks during the day, while employers should revamp how they design their employee lounges (possibly adding a few footstools).

Bottom line: Everyone could benefit if we create an environment in the workplaces and homes of America that allows us to incorporate this important bodily function into our daily lives.

❧ ❧ ❧

Finding Special Moments

I AM A MORNING PERSON. I have always enjoyed rising early, making a pot of coffee, getting the newspaper, and settling down for an hour of quiet time—which I call a time-out.

When I was a child, I remember my mother using time-outs as punishment. However, even then I enjoyed going to my room to think about how I was behaving and what I needed to do "to be a good boy." I enjoyed my time-out then, and I still do, although now I consider a time-out to be a reward rather than a punishment.

Over the years, I have noticed that it has become more and more difficult to set aside those special moments of the day when we can remove ourselves from the hectic, frenetic pace of everyday life. Yet finding time to get away, to reflect, to concentrate, or to just let the mind wander freely is important for our overall health. Studies have shown that reducing stress in daily life significantly reduces the risk of heart attacks or the need for heart surgery.

I remember the days when simply driving to and from work supplied me with the time-out I needed each day. Now, with a beeper strapped to my waist and a cell phone by my side, those days are over. I can be reached anytime, anywhere—even in my car.

It was once believed that the American housewife's life would be less hectic and stressful with the introduction of appliances such as refrigerators, washing machines, dryers, dishwashers, and microwave ovens. They were wrong. Although the advent of modern conveniences may have made many people temporarily more productive and thereby able to free up valuable time, it also increased their workload—because with the extra time, many individuals merely added more chores to their day.

Modern technology has invaded our lives. Reading and answering my e-mail at work and later at home each day may keep me better informed, but it also takes away from the precious time I used to spend reading a book or visiting with friends. The same goes for my beeper, which often keeps me tethered to a nearby phone, although it allows me to be rapidly responsive to the needs of others.

But what about *my* needs?

As a little boy, I recall a time when our family only had one telephone tucked away in a recess in the hall of our home. That one phone was shared by several other families—what we called party lines. Today telephones are in bedrooms, libraries, living rooms, kitchens, and even bathrooms, and often have two or three lines—with call waiting, of course.

This all helps to explain why I love early mornings. No one is awake, the house is quiet, the telephone isn't ringing, the fax machine isn't transmitting its messages, and the computer is dormant. My beeper has not yet been turned on, and I am alone with my coffee, newspaper, and quiet thoughts. It is my daily time-out.

As I grow older, I've noticed the need for more of these daily time-outs, so lately I've started taking a 15-minute stroll with my wife and dog after coming home from the hospital.

I leave all the modern technological and communication devices behind, and walk out my front door a free man. My wife and I exchange news of our day and talk about anything else that's on our minds. It is our time-out together.

As we reenter our home, I cannot help but smile as I notice the three new messages on the answering machine that came in while we were out walking.

Time-out is over—at least until early tomorrow morning.

It's How You End Your Life

YEARS AGO, I developed a philosophy that has often helped me place life's unfolding events into perspective. It is not how you *begin*, but rather how you *finish* your life that's truly important.

Born into this world, we mortals are blueprints of our parents, totally dependent on caretakers for sustenance and survival. Helpless and unaware, we are ushered into childhood, where, for the most part, we are allowed to make few decisions about our environment or surroundings.

Slowly but surely, we dip our toes into the river of adolescence, finding currents of change and turbulence. It is here that we finally understand the feeling of individuality. While it is at this stage in our lives that we yearn for independence and freedom, we are rarely given what we yearn for. Rather, we find that our parents, teachers, and supervisors are watching over us with increased vigor, attempting to fine-tune these important years of growth.

The final years of high school and then college give us the freedom and independence we have sought, only to bring with it the realization that we don't know what we really want. The early years are not truly ours—they are a time when we're being shaped and molded by external factors and circumstances.

As we enter the third decade of our existence, however, another realization sets in. We are beginning to have the opportunity to make decisions that truly affect our lives. We are, in essence, becoming the sum total of our choices. Unfortunately, when we are young and inexperienced, we often make errors.

Choosing the wrong profession, lifestyle, or partner are only a few of the mistakes that we occasionally make. And sometimes, many of us seem to make the same mistakes over and over. However, when we're "young," society seems to overlook these gaffes, with a blanket "been there, done that" attitude, and we are given multiple opportunities to "get it right."

Interestingly, for many, it is not until we are in our 40s that we finally *do* get it right, and just in the nick of time. For when we reach this age, society is less accepting of mistakes that were so easily excused when we were in our 20s and 30s. After all, people in their 40s run governments and huge corporations. It is at this point in our lives that a level of maturity and wisdom begins to develop. It is also at this time that opportunities begin to narrow, and making the correct choices becomes more and more critical in shaping who we are, and how we are eventually going to complete our lives.

It is during the last few decades of our lives that we require loving relationships to a greater extent; as well as prosperity, peace, and tranquility. It is also these later years of our lives that our loved ones and friends will remember as our everlasting legacy. We are honored and remembered more for how we *finish* our life than how we started it.

Presidents Kennedy and Clinton are perfect examples. Kennedy died at the height of his career as a hero. Had he lived and had his personal life become public, he might not have achieved such martyr status. And unfortunately, despite President Clinton's many accomplishments, the scandal he was involved in will forever tarnish him and his presidency.

This philosophy in no way implies that it's not important to make well-thought-out decisions when one is young. Rather, it means that when mistakes *are* made, those in their 20s and 30s should not be so hard on themselves. Time remains for errors to be corrected.

Hopefully, as we age, wisdom also grows, and we become more adept at avoiding the mistakes we once made with abandon while we were young. That wisdom gives us the opportunity to live out the end of our lives in relative peace and harmony.

❧ ❧ ❧

Trust: The Foundation of All Relationships

AS I WALKED INTO THE EXAMINATION ROOM at the hospital, I knew that an important decision needed to be made and that it would be up to me to help my pregnant patient and her family make it.

The patient had been sent from an outlying community hospital because of a serious problem that had recently been diagnosed. Not expecting any pregnancy problems, and planning a routine first birth, my patient had just been told that her unborn child was not growing properly and would probably not be able to withstand the rigors of labor. Our tests confirmed fetal growth restriction, and further tests revealed a very low fetal tolerance to stress. A cesarean section was therefore needed to protect the child's health.

I had been told by the nurses prior to meeting this patient that she and her family were confused about what to do, and, of course, they were anxious and frightened. Briefly introducing myself to the patient and her husband, I explained in considerable detail what was going on and what needed to be done. After a few of their questions were answered, they turned to me and said, "Do what you think is best, Doc. We trust you."

"We trust you" are words that physicians hear often and do not take lightly, for trust is the very foundation of a physician/patient relationship. Despite having just met me, this patient and her husband were willing to allow me to take her to the operating room and, despite inherent risks, perform major abdominal surgery.

I am constantly in awe of this phenomenon. People who probably seek several opinions before selecting a mechanic to fix their ailing car, or who compare prices at numerous stores before buying a household appliance, do not hesitate to immediately concur when one physician explains that a serious medical procedure needs to be performed.

Trust is the single most important factor in all relationships, and when in place, it's a virtue that is highly valued and much appreciated. Trust in some circumstances is acquired almost instantly, as was the case with the patient I mentioned above, who trusted me to perform major surgery after only a few minutes of discussion—and in the same way that I trust the pilot who's about to fly an airplane I've just boarded.

In other situations, trust is not as easily achieved and often takes time to build. New lovers find that issues surrounding trust need nurturing and special emphasis. Children are often required to prove that they can be trusted before being given certain tasks or responsibilities. Yet, no matter how long or short it takes to build, within a very short period of time, trust can be irrevocably lost.

To trust is to relax, and to trust is to be at peace. Doctors work very hard to maintain a patient's unshakable trust. The medical profession's attempts to advocate for patients' needs and rights, to speak openly and honestly concerning health issues, and to place a high priority on confidentiality, are but a few of the ways in which physicians develop and maintain trust between themselves and their patients.

It is this trust that allowed my patient and her husband to feel comfort and peace when they told me to "do what you think is best." I am grateful for that type of trust and can only hope that it is never eroded by the multiple changes that our American health-care system is now undergoing. For trust is at the heart of our work and is the very glue that bonds the doctor/patient relationship.

Trust me—I am a doctor.

The Physician/Patient Bond

I WAS ONLY 21 YEARS OLD the day I started medical school at Vanderbilt University 38 years ago. It was a day I will never forget.

Our class of 52 freshman students put on new, long white coats and took our seats. We were nervous, anxious, naive, and very young as we awaited the arrival of our professor, who was to guide us through a semester of gross anatomy.

Moments later, a tall, silver-haired man entered the room, his starched white coat flowing behind him, his eyes focused and calm as he began to speak. He began by telling us that we were soon to enter the laboratory and receive our cadaver—a human body that we were to dissect and study in excruciating detail.

He explained that when we entered the lab and stood beside this cadaver, we should take a moment of silence and say some special words of gratitude. Our professor told us that we should thank that once-upon-a-time living, breathing human being who had so graciously donated his or her body so that we young students of medicine could have the chance to study human anatomy.

Indeed, it was quite appropriate to offer a word of thanks to Adam (the name I gave my cadaver) that day. In my pursuit of medical knowledge, no greater gift has been given to me. Adam was my first patient, and I was taught to respect him for helping to provide me with the knowledge of all the organs of the human body. I had a moral obligation to treat him with dignity and respect during our time together.

Throughout medical school and beyond, men and women studying the art and science of medicine are constantly reminded of the bond that exists between patient and physician. Through classroom discussions and role modeling, it is branded onto our brains and seared into our souls that our patients' lives are in our hands—and we must never forsake them!

All of these memories flooded back to me recently as I read an article in the *Journal of the American Medical Association* on the subject of professionalism in medical education. A profession was defined as having, among other things, a responsibility to place needs of clients (patients) ahead of any self-interest of the practitioner.

This is what physicians are taught throughout our medical-school education. Classes on bedside manner that focus on understanding who our patients are, what they may be feeling, and how best to talk to them are ongoing. Classes that ask the students to look within themselves to see how they would handle the enormous grief associated with a dying patient are taught. Classes that teach through role-playing how to handle life-crisis issues and how quickly life can change because of illness or death are also a part of our education. We are taught how to look inward and listen outward.

This helps to illustrate why my colleagues are not complaining the loudest about managed care's effect on their annual income. This helps explain why in doctors' lounges and lunchrooms all across this country the issues complained about most have to do with the frustrations in dealing with the managed-care systems as far as treatment of patients is concerned. We resent the intrusion of non-doctors putting themselves between patient and physician, deciding what is appropriate to pay for and what is not.

It is not the loss of income that doctors are moaning about, it's the loss of control of that sacred trust between patient and physician. That helps explain why organized medicine, usually quite conservative in its approach, has actually joined forces with one its most virulent adversaries, American trial lawyers, in agreeing to support a patient's right to sue their HMO.

Our responsibility to place the needs of our patients ahead of our own needs is what we are taught, what we learn, what matters most to us, and what makes our medical field a true profession.

Today, the first-year medical school classes at Vanderbilt still pay tribute to their cadavers in a memorial service conducted at the end of the semester. Students present special readings, sing hymns, and lead a service held in the laboratory. No greater lesson can be given to these young students. The patient's needs—even those patients who are no longer among the living—are paramount, and it is the responsibility of our profession to continue to place those needs above everything else.

Reading the Obit Column

I'M NOT EXACTLY SURE when I started reading the obituary column on a regular basis, but I'm fairly confident that it has only been during the past few years.

This column is not the first item I read each morning, but it is certainly a part on my daily reading agenda. I generally start with the front page of the newspaper and then follow with the op-ed, business, living, sports, and local sections.

When I do get to the obits, the first thing I look for is a familiar name or face, but absent that, I then scan the article for age at time of death. If the deceased is older than, say, 80, I am not quite as troubled as I am if they are closer to my age (61 years). Should they be around this age or worse, younger, a sinking feeling sets in. *Too young,* I think. *That could be me.* And, of course, I then read on to find out all the details. If the cause of death is some terrible disease, I feel a temporary sense of hope. After all, as far as I know, I don't have any diseases.

Automobile accidents, drowning, and other such causes of death also reassure me somewhat, since I drive safely, wear seat belts, and am a very good swimmer. In addition, I do not participate in any type of risky behaviors.

If someone is close to my age, the one cause of death that brings about the most discomfort and creates a feeling of vulnerability as I drink my morning cup of coffee is "sudden, unexpected heart attack." That scenario hits me like a ton of bricks. After all, that *could* be me! Now I must read on. Who was this person, what did he or she do for a living, and who are the loved ones left behind? I stare just a little too long at the accompanying photograph. The person always looks so young and alive.

I suppose there's something to be said for the old statement that upon waking up in the morning, one should first read the obituary column. If your name isn't listed, it's safe to start the day.

A more reflective Morrie Schwarz, the subject of the best-seller *Tuesdays with Morrie,* put it another way. He believed that each night when he went to sleep he died; and each morning as he awoke to another day, he was reborn. Interesting thought, don't you think?

The reading of obituary columns each morning tends to reinforce the belief I've had since my early days in medicine: Each day of our lives is precious and should be celebrated and nurtured. Many people forget this, and that's truly a shame, because it's vital to remember that on any given day, you may be *reading* the obituary column . . . and on the next, you may be *featured* in it.

Our Beloved Sheba

"I'M WORRIED," my wife, Julie, told me. "Dr. Ladd thinks it's an allergic reaction with a secondary infection setting in. He gave me a few prescriptions to fill. I'll talk to you later."

As I placed the phone back into its cradle, I must admit that I felt a pang of concern myself.

Later that evening while taking our daily walk around the neighborhood, Julie and I discussed the diagnosis, treatment, and prognosis, and I felt a little better.

Now lest you think we were talking about my wife's health, we weren't. You see, we were talking about Sheba, our dog, although she seems more like our fourth child. She came into our lives and hearts quite by accident when she was just six weeks old, but the moment we saw her, we knew she had found a home.

Back then, when she was just a puppy, Sheba could only sleep if she was in our room. Separation was almost impossible then, and to this day whenever we leave the house, she has that look on her face that says, "Please take me."

A tail that never stops wagging, a tongue that would lick your hand away if you let it, eyes that reveal much of what she is thinking, and a personality that is warm and cuddly best describes our four-year-old pet. Sheba enjoys riding in the car and taking walks, and she especially loves to snuggle between Julie and me as we sleep.

Needless to say, Sheba brings us a great deal of joy and companionship.

What's interesting is that people who love animals feel pretty much the same way about their own dogs and cats as we feel about Sheba. We regard them as our children, our buddies, our best friends.

Not only that, but we believe that pets function as healers as well. Studies have shown that elderly people who have pets, or who are even exposed to them, cope much better with life's problems than those who do not have this type of contact.

I'm not surprised. I heard about a woman who explained that without her dogs, she would have never been able to handle the grief that enveloped her when her husband passed away. I know of people whose sole companion is their pet. These people are not lonely . . . because they're not alone.

The type of pet makes no difference, although dogs have always been my favorite. There is just something about the way they look at you when you talk to them that endears these animals to me. And no matter what happens, dogs are loyal, always waiting for praise and affection.

Sheba is my sixth dog, and, no offense to the other five, my favorite. Early and effective training was invaluable and allows us to enjoy her that much more. I miss Sheba when she's not with us, and I worry about her when I'm not at home. I love coming home at night to find her standing at the back door, tail wagging a mile a minute.

Yes, Sheba brings Julie and me a great deal of comfort, and I also believe she keeps us just a little bit healthier.

Sheba is fine now, so Julie and I can put our worries aside, but I know there will be a next time. That's why our veterinarian Dr. Ladd's telephone number is right next to our other emergency numbers. After all, Sheba's family, just like the rest of us.

A Proud Profession

LITTLE DID I KNOW that less than 24 hours after I had given a lecture to medical students on how to deliver bad news to patients, a physician I had seen for a cardiac screening test would be giving *me* bad news.

Concerned that my father had suffered his first heart attack at age 60, and knowing that I had problems with increased cholesterol levels, my physician recommended that I undergo a new test called an ultra-fast CT scan. This test could detect calcium deposits in coronary arteries and thereby alert me to the possibility of yet undetected heart disease.

Physicians have often been criticized for the way they deliver bad news to patients and their families. For years, therefore, I have given a two-hour lecture to medical students on how best to handle these extremely sensitive moments.

From "Your test is positive for cancer" to "Your loved one has died," physicians often feel less than properly trained to handle such heart-wrenching interactions. And so, as I left the classroom on the Vanderbilt Medical Center campus that day and drove toward the cardiac testing office, my mind was still focused on how the class had gone.

Being an optimist and having watched my diet, exercised regularly, and taken anti-cholesterol medication for years, I was confident that this test was going to pose no problem for me and I would pass with flying colors.

The cardiologist, whom I had not met before, asked me to join him while he reviewed my test results. The test had only taken a few minutes, and the results had been computerized and placed on a monitor in his office. As if he had just participated in my class on how to tell patients bad news, the cardiologist carefully showed me what was a normal test and what was an abnormal one. He then brought my test result up on the screen. I was stunned. My test looked very much like the abnormal one he had just shown me. It revealed considerable calcium deposits in all three of my coronary vessels.

"Unfortunately, Frank, this isn't good news; although, in many ways, it is not bad news either," he said in a calm and soothing voice. "We really don't know for sure whether this indicates blockage in your coronary arteries; however, a cardiac catheterization can answer that question. If there is blockage, we can open your arteries, possibly saving your life. If no blockage is found, you can relax and know that a heart attack in the near future is quite unlikely. Really, Frank, this is a win-win situation."

I sat there hanging on his every word. Outwardly, I looked calm; however, unknown to this doctor, my mind and pulse were racing. Suddenly, I could not think about the days ahead or the many plans I had on my calendar. My world had come to a temporary halt.

Immediately checking with my personal physician, and a cardiologist who had examined me in the past, plans were made for a cardiac catheterization to be performed two days later.

Cardiac catheterization is considered the gold standard in determining if coronary arteries are open or blocked. By passing a catheter from an artery in my leg into the heart, and injecting dye through the coronary arteries, x-rays could detect whether or not my coronary vessels were blocked and if I needed corrective surgery.

Clearing my calendar for the next few days, I prepared myself, physically as well as emotionally and spiritually. As if a veil had been pulled across my face, I had a difficult time focusing on unrelated matters. Despite being an optimist, I was nonetheless anxious and nervous.

Two days later, I left my home for the hospital where the arteriogram was to be performed. From the moment I arrived to later in the day when I left the hospital to return home,

I was treated by the entire staff of doctors, nurses, technicians, and administrators with a professionalism that constantly kept me calm and reassured. Although still slightly sedated, I listened with interest as my cardiologist told me the good news following the procedure: "Your coronary arteries show no blockage, Frank. You're fine. Congratulations!"

Going from bad news to good news in less than 48 hours, I felt as if I had been on a roller coaster. But I was enormously relieved and felt that the veil had been lifted and I could once again focus on tomorrow.

Those 48 hours demonstrated how wonderfully our medical system can work. From sophisticated medical tests and procedures to sensitive and superb physicians, nurses, technicians, and administrators, I was truly proud of the profession I had chosen as my life's work. It had met all of my expectations.

It is unfortunate that everyone in America cannot expect the same. But I have faith in our medical profession that the day will come when it will meet all of our expectations.

Afterword

I have been a practicing physician for over three decades, and I'm gratified that I chose medicine as my life's work. Working with patients has been the most rewarding aspect of my professional life.

I have learned much from my patients. They have taught me humility, compassion, strength, and purpose. And medicine as a whole has revealed much about the way people handle the trials and tribulations of their lives.

Medicine has also allowed me to understand the human body, the political concerns that surround our profession, and many issues that are truly impossible to explain. Medicine has also offered me the opportunity to participate in the education of young doctors, and given me the privilege of working with some of the most outstanding men and women I have ever met.These are the dedicated individuals who, often facing huge financial burdens and arduous years of study, voluntarily enter the field of medicine to spread understanding, compassion, and health to the world.

You may not know them all, but you do know a few. They "practice" medicine because they are perpetual students, always seeking out better ways to administer their healing techniques.

They are the teachers of the next generation of doctors, ever so carefully nurturing their students' entrance into the honored profession of medicine. They are the researchers, constantly evaluating new ideas, technologies, and treatments to improve the health of their patients.

They are the men and women who sit at a patient's bedside for many sleepless hours, listening, prodding, and encouraging in an effort to heal and bring comfort.

Working side-by-side with my colleagues, I have come to respect and admire the professionals who have dedicated themselves to helping others regain health, and I have seen their anguish when things have not gone well. I have come to understand that these physicians, young and old, care very much about what happens to those under their care.

All in all, I have learned that *doctors cry, too.*

About the *Author*

FRANK H. BOEHM, M.D., is a professor of obstetrics and gynecology and the director of maternal/fetal medicine at Vanderbilt University Medical School in Nashville, Tennessee.
He is also chairman of the Vanderbilt University Medical
Center Ethics Committee.

Dr. Boehm is a graduate of Vanderbilt Medical School
and the Yale-New Haven Hospital internship and residency
program. He is a specialist in high-risk pregnancy, called peri-
natology, and is recognized worldwide in the specialized field
of fetal monitoring.

Dr. Boehm has authored more than 200 scientific publications and has co-edited a major textbook. He is a member
of the Vanderbilt Chapter of Alpha Omega Alpha, was awarded
the Mead Johnson Award for Graduate Teaching, and was
named Man of the Year by CABLE, an organization of
Nashville business and professional women.

In addition, from 1992 to 1999, Dr. Boehm was listed in
The Best Doctors in America, a referral guide of the nation's
finest physicians based on peer nominations and recommen-
dations. In August 1997, *Good Housekeeping* listed Dr. Boehm
among the nation's best doctors for women in the field of peri-
natology, and in the year 2000, he received the Award for
Excellence in Clinical Teaching from Vanderbilt University
School of Medicine's faculty.

Dr. Boehm has served on numerous national committees, presently serves as a reviewer of major scientific publications in his field, and acts as an editorial consultant for a number of prestigious medical journals. In addition, he has spoken throughout the United States, Canada, Mexico, Europe, and the Middle East. He currently co-authors a column called "Healing Words" in *The Tennessean*, a Nashville newspaper.

Dr. Boehm has three children: Todd, Tommy, and Catherine; and a granddaughter, Riley Isabel. He resides with his wife, Julie, in Nashville and Boca Raton.

We hope you enjoyed this Hay House book. If you'd like to receive our online catalog featuring additional information on Hay House books and products, or if you'd like to find out more about the Hay Foundation, please contact:

Hay House, Inc., P.O. Box 5100, Carlsbad, CA 92018-5100
(760) 431-7695 or (800) 654-5126
(760) 431-6948 (fax) or (800) 650-5115 (fax)
www.hayhouse.com® • www.hayfoundation.org

———

Published in Australia by: Hay House Australia Pty. Ltd.,
18/36 Ralph St., Alexandria NSW 2015
Phone: 612-9669-4299 • *Fax:* 612-9669-4144
www.hayhouse.com.au

Published in the United Kingdom by: Hay House UK, Ltd.,
The Sixth Floor, Watson House, 54 Baker Street, London W1U 7BU
Phone: +44 (0)20 3927 7290 • *Fax:* +44 (0)20 3927 7291
www.hayhouse.co.uk

Published in India by: Hay House Publishers India,
Muskaan Complex, Plot No. 3, B-2, Vasant Kunj, New Delhi 110 070
Phone: 91-11-4176-1620 • *Fax:* 91-11-4176-1630
www.hayhouse.co.in

———

**Access New Knowledge.
Anytime. Anywhere.**

Learn and evolve at your own pace
with the world's leading experts.

www.hayhouseU.com

Free e-newsletters
from Hay House, the Ultimate
Resource for Inspiration

Be the first to know about Hay House's free downloads, special offers, giveaways, contests, and more!

 Get exclusive excerpts from our latest releases and videos from *Hay House Present Moments*.

 Our *Digital Products Newsletter* is the perfect way to stay up-to-date on our latest discounted eBooks, featured mobile apps, and Live Online and On Demand events.

 Learn with real benefits! *HayHouseU.com* is your source for the most innovative online courses from the world's leading personal growth experts. Be the first to know about new online courses and to receive exclusive discounts.

 Enjoy uplifting personal stories, how-to articles, and healing advice, along with videos and empowering quotes, within *Heal Your Life*.

Sign Up Now!

Get inspired, educate yourself, get a complimentary gift, and share the wisdom!

Visit www.hayhouse.com/newsletters to sign up today!

Printed in the United States
By Bookmasters